TALKING TO CHINA

TALKING TO CHINA

The Future of UK–China Relations

Kerry Brown

agenda
publishing

To Carma Eliot, a true exemplar of the best of UK–Chinese cooperation, and Carolyn and Doug Scott, for their friendship and support over the years.

First published in 2025 by Agenda Publishing

Agenda Publishing Limited
PO Box 185
Newcastle upon Tyne
NE20 2DH
www.agendapub.com

ISBN 978-1-78821-846-7

British Library Cataloguing-in-Publication Data
A catalogue record for this book is available from the British Library

Typeset by JS Typesetting Ltd, Porthcawl, Mid Glamorgan
Printed and bound in the UK by 4edge

EU GPSR authorised representative:
Logos Europe, 9 rue Nicolas Poussin, 17000 La Rochelle, France
contact@logoseurope.eu

Contents

知彼知己，百戰不殆

Know yourself and your opponent: then you will fight a
hundred battles with success
Sun Tzu, *The Art of War*

Preface

When, in 2019, *The Future of UK–China Relations* was published, the clouds that were starting to gather on the horizon of UK–China relations since 2017 had started to thicken. Within a year, a storm broke out, and almost every aspect of the relationship was either disrupted, distorted, or simply destroyed. The first Trump presidency, from 2017, pushed for a harder, more deal orientated relationship with China to rebalance what the White House claimed were unfair trade surpluses in Beijing's favour. Europe was drawn into the argument, being whipped into line by the United States when it tried to pursue what it regarded as a more pragmatic, self-interested path in the summer of 2018. Despite key European leaders visiting Trump's officials, and courting the then Chinese Premier Li Keqiang on a visit to their continent, they had to draw in behind the US and support its demands for a better trade deal.[1] Around the same time as the US and China finally reached agreement on better market access in early 2020, the Europeans finally agreed a joint Common Agreement on Investment after seven years of argument. That ended up failing to be ratified the next year by the European Parliament because of sanctions placed by the Chinese government on some of its members (a retaliation for sanctions placed on some of their officials connected with the Xinjiang issue).

The desire for a new, more balanced relationship was hardly something incompatible with the "Golden Era" approach that Britain had attempted after the State Visit of Xi Jinping to Britain in 2015. The underlying rationale of that, as the then Chancellor of the Exchequer George Osborne made clear, was simply for Britian to get more out of the Chinese economy. Speaking in Shanghai in September that year, Osborne declared:

> Increasing exports, boosting tourism and attracting the brightest and the best students to the UK will drive job creation and productivity growth in our economy. It's why it's such an important part of our long term economic plan. Both Britain and China also recognise the importance of rebalancing our economies. It's another way we can partner each other on the journey ahead.[2]

Partnership and travelling together, the notion of balance and harmony – underpinning these was a recognition that despite investment, technology transfer and multiple dialogues and offerings of advice, there was still a feeling that things between the two nations were suboptimal – and a sense in London that overall, the results of the bilateral cooperation were underwhelming.

The first reports of a new virus from the central city of Wuhan at the start of 2020 (even though the earliest signs of a persistent, and potentially deadly, dry cough with feverish symptoms had been at the end of 2019) resulted in a full-blown pandemic. Borders closed. Lockdowns were imposed. Governments across the globe saw their health systems overwhelmed by numbers of people infected. Casualties soared. The political impact of all of this was quick, and severe. China was accused of being late in giving data about the problem to the World Health Organisation.[3] Australia and then others demanded an enquiry into why the problem had started in the first place – something the Chinese rejected with fury. As Covid-19, as it came to be called, spread globally, anger in the US and elsewhere at how the Chinese government had managed the start of the problem escalated, with many accusing it of secrecy and dishonesty. This culminated in President Trump labelling the issue "the China virus" in a tweet.[4] A rise of attacks on people of Asian heritage in the US, Europe and elsewhere was one of the more lamentable outcomes of this. But the general lack of direct person-to-person contact as planes were grounded and borders closed, and the massive costs lockdowns incurred, along with the rise in fatalities as those afflicted with the disease died, marked a watershed moment.

In the end, it was unsurprising that Prime Minister Rishi Sunak declared at a speech in at the Lord Mayor's Banquet in London on 29 November 2022 that the "Golden Era" was over.[5] It was remarkable that the idea had survived as long as it had. Piled on to the impact of the pandemic was the final exit from the European Union by Britain after over four decades of membership in 2020, and general political turbulence in Britain in which, in 2022, three prime ministers served, one of them for the shortest term ever.

China's actions and policies also contributed to the general collapse of public views towards the country amongst the British. The mass incarceration of predominantly people of Uyghur ethnicity in the Xinjiang region of the country became a major issue, and one that inspired some members of parliament to label the actions "genocide". Hong Kong remained a particular challenge, with the passing of a sweeping new National Security Law in 2020 which was then used against democracy activists and political figures. High-profile cases like that of newspaper owner and businessman Jimmy Lai drew attention to the general erosion of civil liberties and freedom of speech in the country. One of the most impactful events over the post-2020 period between Britain and China was the passing of a new regulation allowing those in the city to apply for British National Overseas status, move to the UK , and then have an accelerated pathway to citizenship. Under this scheme, by the end of October 2024, more than 150,000 people came to settle in Britain.[6] That inevitably irritated Beijing, as well as any other signs that Britain, a quarter of a century after relinquishing control of the territory, was still trying to involve itself in its affairs.

The one word therefore that describes the situation of UK–China relations at the end of 2024, the time of writing, is "complex". From China's diplomatic (and possible covert military) support for the Russians in their war on Ukraine, to claims that through the United Front Work Department the Chinese were actively engaged in espionage in Britain, links on almost every level became more conflicted and difficult. Symptomatic of this was the fact that when newly elected Labour Prime Minister Keir Starmer met with Xi Jinping at the G20 in Rio in November 2024, this was the first bilateral conference at this level for seven years.

That complexity is well captured by a document which, while not specifically focused on China, placed the challenges of crafting a sensible, rational UK policy towards this country as one of its key themes – the "Integrated Review", undertaken by the British Cabinet Office, and issued first in 2021, and then revised again in 2023. Recognizing the reality of systemic competition sitting beside the imperative to work on global issues like environment and artificial intelligence (AI), the review stated that:

> We will update the UK's approach to China to keep pace with the evolving and epoch-defining challenge it poses to the international order. First, we will increase our national security protections in those areas where Chinese Communist Party actions pose a threat to our people, prosperity and security. Second, we will deepen our cooperation and increase alignment with both our core allies and a wider group of partners. Third, we will engage directly with China bilaterally and in international fora so that we leave room for open, constructive and predictable relations: diplomacy is a normal part of state-to-state business, and supports the national interest. We will double funding to build China capabilities across government to better understand China and allow us to engage confidently where it is in our interests to do so.[7]

That sense of a relationship that was important, unavoidable, and way more complicated than could be captured in the more sunny, straightforward optimistic language of the "Golden Era" is well expressed in this statement. The sense that Britain needed to know China better raised the question of what its knowledge levels had been like before and what constituted improvement, along with how to bring this about. As this book will argue later, that question of what constituted good knowledge, and how best to acquire this, has never been satisfactorily answered.

One of the perennial mysteries of the UK–China relationship is what the British actually think about China deep down – if anything at all. What sort of sentiment and attitude do they have towards this country? In a discussion in late 2024 with one official from the British government who had dealt with this issue for some years, they stated that all the polling and evidence they had was often complex and conflicting, and varied across age groups, regions, educational background, etc. The one constant between all these was the view that China was somehow unknowable and very different. The pandemic certainly made China seem nearer and more relevant to the UK – although not in a positive way. Perhaps that was why a YouGov poll in 2022 said that only 13 per cent of British people had a positive view of China, and more than 70 per cent a negative one.[8] Emotions ran higher than before in public discourse on China, with stories about claims of Chinese espionage in Britain, and the first threads of something almost akin to McCarthyism with British characteristics, where almost anyone with links to the People's Republic were made to defend themselves, and had suspicion cast on them. The US experienced this more intensely, but for Britain, with the work of groups like the China Research Group, working for MPs, this heightened public awareness of China as a problem was a new development.

Since 2019, I have benefited from something that I was able to do during a year's sabbatical from 2022 to 2023 from King's College, London, where I am chair of Chinese Studies and direct an institute focusing on the study and research of contemporary China. Over that time, I researched and then wrote a full-length comprehensive history of Britain's relations with China, going back to the time of earliest recorded contact in the sixteenth century. The letters that Elizabeth I wrote to the Wan Li emperor advocating trading links were never delivered, because of the lack of any real shipping or land routes between the two powers that were reliable. Even so, when the Tudor monarch declared that the two places had much need of each other, it was an aspiration which was to echo down the decades and centuries. One thing that reading a huge amount of material about this history, some of it in archives in Britain, or online, made abundantly clear was that the impact on each other was huge, but never fully recognized. The British started drinking tea imported from China from the 1650s, with so much import revenue coming from this single source a century later it was enough to fund the Royal Navy. Porcelain and silk were two other important imports, one of them copied successfully by the likes of Wedgewood and Spode, and the other significantly enhancing British sense of fashion. There was the impact too of Chinese ideas on aesthetics in terms of architecture, gardening and even furniture (Thomas Chippendale the furniture maker produced a workbook on Chinese style and chairs and tables in the mid-eighteenth century). Chinoiserie impacted on wallpaper design, literature, and manifested itself in such expressions of exotic difference as the Brighton Pavilion. In the other direction, China was influenced, sometimes by persuasion, but all too often by force, by British notions of industry, technology, governance and law. By the end of the nineteenth century, through the Imperial Maritime Customs service under the redoubtable Ulsterman Robert Hart, a largely British founded and run entity was responsible for about a third of the Qing government revenue.

Since 1900, one might argue that the British China story has been one of slow retreat. The twentieth century saw the collapse of the Qing, the rise to influence in China of other powers like the Russians, and, most significantly, and tragically, the Japanese. By the time of the Communist victory in 1949, Britain was a less important power to China than the Soviet Union, or the US. But unlike these two, Britain maintained a constant diplomatic presence in China over the next decades, largely to safeguard its interests in Hong Kong. Unlike any other major power from the political West, Britain never ceased speaking to China and interacting with it. The issue in the end, as my research showed, was not so much that today we did not know much about each other. It was more that we knew a lot, but often chose, or happened, to forget it.

This book hopes to make an accessible contribution to the better understanding and framing of a major relationship for the UK, one which will remain unavoidable, even if complex and vexing in the years to come. For all the increase in discussion and commentary about UK–China relations, whether from politicians, officials, businesspeople, experts, lobbyists, and media pundits, a characteristic from 2020 to 2024 was the appearance of a new set of voices whose strong views about China were often not backed up by any direct experience of the place, or any signs that they had devoted much time to sustained effort to understand it. The general debate about China became like a raucous echo chamber, where the main aim seemed to be to outdo previous statements about how serious a threat China was to the UK. As this book makes clear, however, one of the great disadvantages of taking this approach is that it gives Britain the illusion it has more choices than it actually does. Economically, geopolitically, environmentally, technologically, China remains an unavoidable partner. There is nothing new about this situation, if this was any comfort. It has been the situation for much of the previous four centuries. What has changed – and dramatically – is the asymmetry of power between the two. From centuries of relative dominance, today Britain is in the position of being the smaller economy, the weaker military power, and a far less powerful geopolitical actor than China. Therein lies the China conundrum for the UK: how to influence a power that one cannot avoid, and yet one seldom agrees with and has very limited leverage or powers of influence over.

Setting the scene: the British China story

It was one of those large public debating festivals held usually during the warm months in Britain. A packed schedule of events over two days, addressing issues from the US election to the impact of artificial intelligence – a smorgasbord of argumentation and intellectual manoeuvring by speakers and their audiences. Panels with invited experts on specific themes spoke for a few minutes each and then there were moderated question and answer sessions with the audience. I was glad to have been invited just as an academic attendee. Academics were at least spared the full onslaught of public indignation and rage because we were regarded as experts present to give balance. Polemicists, controversialists, politicians, and self-publicizers were not so lucky. But then, in an odd way, brutal treatment by their audiences seemed to be what they were there for. They had the philosopher Friedrich Nietzsche's famous dictum engraved on their hearts: what didn't kill them was going to make them stronger; they seemed to be there to survive and then get more powerful.

Academics are supposedly custodians of neutrality. That is our claim about ourselves at least. And these days, the title "Professor" still (just about!) gives some pause for thought and restraint on whomever you are facing publicly and grants a little bit of mercy. My session was about the impact of the rise of China. The argument I used was one that I had deployed at similar events throughout Europe and the rest of the world over the previous months and years: like it or not, China was going to be part of our global economic future and probably our geopolitical and social one. Even if we were not going to it, it was coming to us – through investment, finance, students and tourists. This was a moment of historic change. For the first time in modern history, a power with a profoundly different cultural background and a very different set of values (ones that

I shall spell out in more detail later) was about to take centre stage. We (and throughout this work, when I use the word "we" I am referring to constituencies in the UK) needed to adjust our mindsets, revise our vocabularies, and reset our standard maps of the world. This was not an issue on which we could adopt discrete neutrality. Opposition to China or attempts to exclude it was futile. This wasn't about its political model but about the fact that it was a country that encompassed a fifth of the human race. As far back as 1968, in an article in *Foreign Affairs*, the then US presidential candidate, Richard Nixon, wrote that the world had no moral or intellectual right to exclude this large segment of humanity from the global community. Later, as president, he famously proceeded to put this into action by effecting a rapprochement with the People's Republic in 1972. That argument, in very different ways and in transformed circumstances, was no less true half a century later. The main question now was just what sort of space and what kinds of shared future could we, whether British, European or North American, create with a country loaded with ambition and with the sense that its moment of just restoration, after a modern history full of challenges and suffering, was finally coming good.[1]

The audience that came to the debates that day, as almost all audiences I have spoken to in the UK, was polite and thoughtful. They listened to news and analysis of the fundamental rearrangement of the power structures and realignment of geopolitical forces in the world they were living in with an almost preternatural calm. There was a lack of emotion or anything approaching concern or fear. Similar speeches, when I had been based in Sydney for three years from 2012, usually evinced much more visceral and urgently anxious reactions, testifying to the differences in sentiment and public attitudes amongst the local audience there who saw the influence of China on their country as more immediate and far more consequential. But in the UK, at least at that time, it seemed the ethos of "keep calm and carry on" extended even to an issue as potentially disruptive as this.

What was striking about this lack of emotional response that day was that this was clearly not due to the particular intrinsic qualities or dispositions of the people in the audience. This was not an indifferent, unmoved group of people. On different subjects, they were more than willing to express deep, often divided feelings. A debate on the UK and the European Union in one of the neighbouring rooms nearly ended in a riot, with participants so deeply polarized they may as well have come from different planets. But the most fractious debate, which was so well attended I was only able to squeeze into the back of the room to listen, was about recycling. Enraged speeches from the floor decried local council incompetence in refuse management. An elderly gentleman went puce red when describing the amount of time he needed to sort out rubbish into separate categories only to read in the *Daily Mail* that it had been dumped in the same landfill. One environmentalist on the panel was screamed at for saying "Your children will blame you for not doing anything about this". What was staggering was that the debates were not about disagreements over scientific evidence for climate change – everyone at least seemed to accept there was a problem. The anger was more about some nebulous idea of a mendaciously incompetent state, which was doing its best to irritate people and then claim it was there to help when it was clearly consistently failing.

That experience seemed to me highly indicative of the attitude in the UK towards China for much of the period up to around 2018. In Britian, China continued to occupy a niche position. Issues like Hong Kong, the status of Tibet, and, increasingly from around 2017 with the first reports of camps in the Xinjiang region of China detaining people of Uyghur ethnicity, did receive coverage. So too did trade matters, like the amounts of investment into the UK from the new place recognized as a global economic powerhouse. But compared to the passions generated during the debate about European Union membership by Britain up to the referendum in 2016, or the amount of engagement that the 2016 and then 2020 election in the US attracted in British media (social, print and other) China and matters related to it only made sporadic appearances.

That at least was the way things looked when I wrote about the UK–China relationship in the 2010s. Then I wanted to answer why it was that there was this lack of emotion, which almost verged on indifference, towards something which would seem to merit much more engagement? In many ways, what happened after 2018, as alluded to in the introduction, answered that question. Either through being affected by the rising tide of anxiety and antagonism to China in the US under the first Trump presidency, or because of the impact of the Covid-19 pandemic and the clear links it had to origination in Wuhan, many British noticed China having an impact on them, and started to express a view about the place as never before. The debate about this issue in the UK became far more fractious and heated. To be fair this was true about a number of other matters, from wearing masks to protect against infection to having vaccinations. But for the British, the appearance of public figures from all political parties who were willing to express views about China, some of them very strongly negative, was striking. The question for this book is to what extent this marks a radical change or whether it is simply a phase before Britain returns to the posture of general indifference that it had occupied before around 2020. Are we in a new paradigm, or returning to the default before the abnormality of the "Golden Era"?

The situation has certainly grown more complicated in the decade since the bold announcement of that golden age, something which is covered in the next chapter. But one thing Britain can definitely do to manage its new position facing a complex issue is to understand itself better – and that means having a better grasp of its own China story. Chinese under Xi Jinping have certainly embraced this notion of having narratives and stories by which to understand themselves, and their role in the world. The state news agency Xinhua indeed called Xi "the storyteller in chief". What soft power efforts they have made under his leadership have largely asserted, more directly and proactively, a sense of Chinese cultural confidence and of coherent national identity. That is built on a redemptive story of modern history, where China has been on a pathway travelling away from suffering and unjust treatment at the hands of colonial, modernizing powers (of which Britain ranks amongst the most significant) in the nineteenth and early twentieth centuries towards a better future. Making China Great Again has been the mission of the Chinese Communist Party since 1949 and given it a new source of legitimacy in the twenty-first century. The Party has vowed under Xi never again to allow the country it governs to be beholden to outsiders and vulnerable to their bullying and coercion. Whatever the historic veracity of this story (it is one in which China itself and most of its previous leaders are largely exonerated from any blame for what happened to the country) it is one that has huge emotional traction in the country today.

BRITAIN'S CHINA STORY

Britain has no strong corresponding story to tell of its specific history with China. There are many reasons for this. One is that such a story is part of a larger tale of British imperialism from the seventeenth century onwards, a subject mired in controversy and argument. The second is that at least for the majority of British, while knowledge of empire up to a degree is common, China occupied a somewhat niche and complex space – never fully colonized, run as what some call an "informal empire" in the late Victorian era, but nowhere near as prominent and important as India where the links were extensive, direct – and expensive! Finally, there is a general lack of intellectual investment in knowing this history because it is sometimes regarded as too difficult and specialist. In many ways, the story of Britain's relations with China, for most British who know something about this, is a palimpsest, where landmark events like the First and Second Anglo-Chinese Wars of the nineteenth century, and the Boxer Rebellion at the dawn of the twentieth, and then the general issue of Hong Kong, stand out from a generally blurry background – partly acknowledged and understood but largely in a context where much is obscured by darkness or a covering veil.

Despite this, the British story of its links with China is rich, and rewarding to understand. It goes back to the Tudor period, and has passed through several phases, and involved a cast of different actors. It is a history worth having some general conception of in order to frame the discussion in the rest of this short book. So first I shall outline at least the main phases the relationship has been through, then draw up some of the key characteristics of British policy towards China over that history, and finally address the question of what has changed about the situation today to make it very different from what existed in the past.

The establishment on the final day of 1599 of the East India Company (EIC) in London as the principle (indeed for India and China the only) means of British trading with the world east of Europe marked the start of a concerted effort to get into the lucrative trade in spices, silk and other goods from the Far East that the Dutch and Portuguese were enjoying. In a haunting echo of the situation over four centuries later in the Brexit era, Britain's arguments and fights with continental Europe in the final years of the Elizabethan reign meant looking to other markets and other

5

opportunities further afield made business and strategic sense. That is what Britain did – a sort of prototype of the "Global Britain" notion that took hold after 2016. A trading post was set up in Hirado, Japan, in 1612 by members of the EIC to try to establish markets in the Far East. The first proper trade mission was sent, though wholly of private businesspeople, in the 1630s. By 1680, British trade interests were being run from Amoy (today's Xiamen) on the coast of southeast China. But it was not until the eighteenth century that a more concerted effort to get trade flows going into China settled on the one place that was allowed by the then governing Qing court – Canton, today's Guangzhou. There, from 1715, a so-called factory (more like a warehouse and workshop for goods) was run, with British traders trying to source from China for export and sell goods into the country.

The first two centuries of Britain's links with China were solely about trade. The people forging these links were merchants and sailors, largely people without sophisticated education, whose motives were simply to benefit financially, and who communicated with the Chinese they dealt with either by Pidgin English, or rudimentary Portuguese (the one language understood by Chinese who were dealing with international trade then). This was not an easy relationship, and it failed to deliver the kinds of returns the EIC and private traders wanted. But by the 1780s, the sheer quantity of tea alone shipped to Britain and the desire to try to sell more goods to the Chinese meant the government became involved. Under Prime Minister William Pitt the Younger's chief advisor Henry Dundas, a formal government embassy led by the distinguished diplomat Lord George Macartney was sent in 1793–4. This marks the second phase of the relationship, one where there was an attempt by the British to have more official links, met by a concerted campaign by the Chinese to reject such links and simply maintain low-level, transactional connections. Macartney's embassy was a failure, though it created a whole new level of knowledge and understanding of China for the British public. This is what we might now recognize as the first attempts to have knowledge about this place, rather than vague feelings and notions about it.

By 1839, this situation had become deeply frustrating for almost all parties. A generation of British traders like William Jardine and James Matheson, had sought to address the imbalances arising from endless exporting of tea and other goods out of China with no corresponding trade into the country by engaging in a massive, mostly contraband, but hugely lucrative trade in opium sourced in India and sold into the Chinese market illegally. While commercially solving the fiscal issue, it created widespread, lamentable social issues through the addiction it gave rise to. Things were compounded by the fact that the EIC's monopoly on the China tea trade ended in 1833, meaning that the country as a market became far more attractive and open, at least in theory, to others. The impediments and restrictions now were on the Chinese side, who were imposing barriers to free trade. Things came to a head when the Chinese appointed an official, Lin Zexu, in 1838 to clamp down on the opium smuggling. An initially reluctant British government under Lord Palmerston embarked on a violent war to counteract this. Superiority particularly in naval and gun technology meant that the first Anglo-Chinese War of 1839–42 ended in a comprehensive British victory. Hong Kong island was ceded to Britain in perpetuity, and a number of treaty ports were opened for trade. British representatives from the government were allowed in the country. Arguments over Chinese non-compliance with these agreements resulted in a second war from 1856 to 1860, the main result of which was a subsequent British victory (although this time with French and other allies taking part), and even greater influence in China. This marks the phase of maximum involvement, where, despite the presence of Germany, France, Japan, America and other nations, Britain accounted for the bulk of trade and investment, and had a huge role in the running of the Chinese financial system. The Hong Kong Shanghai Bank, set up in the early 1860s, typified this, acting in many ways like a bank for the British state as it funded the building of railways, mines and factories across the country.

The collapse of the Qing dynasty in 1911–12, partly as a result of these constant infractions by outsiders but largely from internal issues, marked the moment when Britain started its long retreat. While China was an ally in the First World War from 1917, the rise of Chinese nationalism, the competition from powers like Japan and Russia, and the distraction of issues in Europe over the late 1920s into the 1930s meant that Britain became a less comprehensive power in China, and finally by the end of the Second World War only remained significant largely through its continuing interests in Hong Kong. This issue alone meant that when the Communists achieved their dramatic victory over the Nationalists in 1949 and came to power, Britain recognized the new regime even though other key allies like the US and other Europeans did not. It had representatives in Beijing even as its companies were forced to close their interests there. The Maoist period was a tough one, with the British legation attacked by Red Guards during the Cultural Revolution in 1967, and many of its staff abused and manhandled. But in 1972, as a result of China rather than Taiwan finally being made a member of the United Nations, and the US rapprochement with Beijing, Britain upgraded its relations to ambassadorial status.

The era from the 1970s to 1997 can be characterized as one where most bilateral effort went into resolving the final status of Hong Kong. While the island had been ceded in perpetuity, over 90 per cent of the city was on leases secured over the latter part of the nineteenth century which had a set time period. Most of these were due to expire in 1997. That necessitated the British prime minister from 1979, Margaret Thatcher, sanctioning negotiations with China to resolve what would happen after this. Hong Kong had developed into a key international finance centre, run with a very different economic model and with a wholly different social and political feel than China (even though it was never a full democracy, but run as a colony with most decision-making power residing with the UK-appointed Governor and their team). Ideas about extending the leases were soon dismissed by the Chinese. After torturous negotiations, a final deal was done whereby under a "one country, two systems" framework, Hong Kong was allowed for a period of 50 years after 1997 to enjoy "a high degree of autonomy", running its own affairs, having its own currency, setting its own interest rates, and so on. On that basis, and despite some final arguments in Chris Patten's years as the last Governor (1992–97), Hong Kong reverted to Chinese rule.

From 1997, we arrive at the final phase of the UK–China relationship – until today. One where, with the resolution of the issue of Hong Kong, Britian was able to concentrate on engagement. When Tony Blair was elected prime minister only months before the retrocession in May 1997, I remember joining the British Foreign and Commonwealth Office and working, for a year, in the China Section. The new ethos was about enhancing our relationship, putting the past issues aside – in some senses attempting a prototype golden age. Investment and educational exchanges were tried, a State Visit by the Chinese president,

Jiang Zemin, happened in 1999 – the first time ever that the most senior leader of China had visited Britain. Bit by bit links between Britain and China increased, through events like the Beijing Olympics in 2008, and the Shanghai Expo of 2010. It was never huge numbers but seldom had British people travelled so much to China, and seen China on their news and in the media. That era culminated in the announcement of the "Golden Era" – covered in the next chapter.

HISTORY LESSONS

When we look at this history, what do we learn about the fundamental tramlines of British policy towards China over the centuries? Are there any striking characteristics or features? One thing that is remarkable is that Britain when it had most influence in China, in the late nineteenth century, had a policy that was not so much about what it wanted China to be, but what it did not want it to be. The main aim of policy was to avoid China becoming too powerful and assertive that it pushed back against British interests. But at the same time, it also did not want China to be so weak that it fell. This is typified by the Second Anglo-Chinese War, a brutal and mean-spirited venture, which is best remembered today for the appalling sacking of the Old Summer Palace in Beijing by British and (it shouldn't be forgotten) French troops. The aim of that war was to force China to stop pushing back against British and other foreign demands, and to acquiesce to a new set of treaty obligations and greater openness to British trade. But the war happened as the Qing itself was engaged in an existential fight with the Taiping rebellion that had been raging for most of the last decade. While Britain originally regarded the Taipings, with their promotion of an esoteric form of Christianity, as potential allies, they soon came to view them as disruptive and threatening. They supported the Qing in its final quelling of this insurgency, and while their contribution was less decisive than claimed immediately afterwards, it made clear that Britian wanted a "Goldilocks China" – a place that was suitable and amenable to British commercial needs, but not one that was able to reject them, nor that would need a large amount of support and management. Having fought against the Chinese government when it was rejecting their demands and acting too independently, within a few years it was propping up the regime for fear its dissolution would threaten its own interests in the country.

Alongside this was the issue of values. One of the fascinating, long-standing characteristics of British (and to some extent European) approaches to relations with China was that commerce, and tangible forms of trade and business, were always placed before issues that promoted values. Again, the period of about 50 years between 1850 and 1900, when Britain was at its peak of influence in China, is illustrative. By 1890, Britain's largest consular diplomatic network existed in China, with posts from Kashgar on the edges of the empire in the northwest, to Xiamen, and Chengdu far in the southwest and southeast. This network clashed consistently with the wave of protestant missionaries allowed to come to the country after the treaty changes in the early 1860s allowed religious proselytizing. Their work was regarded as distracting and meddlesome by the British government officials, who took a dim view of what they regarded as the naivety of preachers and pastors now coming to convert. The fact that they achieved very little success in terms of conversions was another issue. The attempts by well-meaning but often zealous missionaries to bring enlightenment to Chinese sometimes ended up in tragicomedy, with one of the converts introduced to Queen Victoria in the 1860s ending up as a thief. Less comic was the Boxer Rebellion which was ignited by the brutal murder of British Christian activists in the countryside at the very end of 1899. With so much influence and power, British state and company policy towards China at the end of the nineteenth century was about preserving its direct trade interests, and not rocking an often unstable boat. Mass conversion of Chinese was regarded as unlikely, and potentially deeply disruptive. Nor, as has often been noted, were the British in their colonial rule over Hong Kong that invested in producing any form of democracy there. Attempts to bring about a more participatory form of administration championed by the Governor after restoration of British rule at the end of the Japanese occupation in the Second World War were stymied by a powerful combination of business interests in the city, and the mandarins back in Whitehall. The reforms were never implemented, and only when the last Governor was in place were there moves from 1992 to bring about more meaningful changes – too late in the day to be continued after 1997 when Beijing almost immediately scrapped them.

By the third decade of the twenty-first century, more than four centuries into the British China story, what has changed? Fundamentally, in four structural areas, there are now immense shifts, ones where a relationship that was always asymmetrical and unbalanced has continued, but with the upper hand decisively changing from the British to the Chinese. Economically, geopolitically, militarily and technologically, for most of their shared history, Britain has been the stronger power and was able to achieve its aims in and with China through being preeminent in these areas. But from the turn of the twenty-first century, a major shift has occurred. In all of these domains, China is now ahead of Britain – in some cases far ahead. That has left much of the historic memory of British relations with China stranded in a new context. In effect, the language and attitude that the British still often display towards China haunted by this memory of so many years of having the upper hand is now out of kilter with reality. Britain no longer has the leverage, the power, the moral high ground (if it ever did) and the diplomatic or political authority – at least on its own – to speak to China and expect it do things that Britain regards as right, or in its interests. It has to persuade and argue, not assert and demand.

China had an economy half the size of Britain's in 1997 when reversion of Hong Kong occurred. Hong Kong at that time was a quarter the size of the whole mainland Chinese gross domestic product. By 2005, as a result of the immense contribution to its growth that entry to the World Trade Organisation made five years before, China drew ahead of Britain. By 2024 its economy was five times the size of the UK's. Of the world's top ten banks according to market capitalization, five were from China – none from Britain. Britain didn't even figure in the list of 120 countries where China was the largest trading partner.

Geopolitically, China is now sitting at the centre of what many claim is an alternative world order. In the Belt and Road Initiative (BRI), it has a series of partnerships across the Global South in particular. With the Asian Infrastructure Investment Bank (AIIB) China has set up a rival of the Asian Development Bank (although in practice the two have since worked with each other on some projects), an entity that, to US displeasure, Britain joined in 2015. With these moves, China has been accused of contesting the global consensus created after the Second World War and the Bretton Woods meeting that saw the foundation of multilateral collaboration entities like the World Bank and the International Monetary Fund by running parallel entities that to some degree compete with these, even as China remains involved and active in them. This ability to sit both inside and outside the current global order means that China like Britain sits on the UN Security Council as one of the Permanent Five members even as it builds the BRI. It belongs to the G20, but now also runs a forum for its relations in Africa, Latin America and the Middle East. It is a different kind of network, but China is now part of a configuration of partnerships that is more extensive than that of Britain.

In terms of military assets, with spending on defence second only to that of the United States, China has capability that easily outreaches Britain's. It has two aircraft carriers and is building a third. It has the world's largest navy in terms of numbers of vessels, a process that only started in the 1980s, but today means that it can project power around its maritime borders, sending its fleet deeper and deeper into the Pacific. The Chinese army is behind the British only in the sense that Britain has seen more combat experience than China over the last half a century. But in terms of current capacity, China is far ahead, both in conventional, nuclear and unconventional forces.

Finally, in terms of technology, in the twenty-first century China has steadily, but dramatically, pulled ahead. It has an increasing number of universities attaining top global rankings, even as British ones largely go in the other direction. It committed £340 billion to research and development in 2024. The UK in the same year devoted only £20 billion. From AI to quantum physics, life sciences, even the production of stealth fighter jets, China produces more new technology, and its universities now outrank British ones in the authorship of peer-reviewed articles.

In the space of a generation, the tables have been reversed, with a completeness that is disarming and staggering. From a period in which British policy towards China in the early years of engagement after 1997 was about promoting rule of law, open markets, privatization, village democracy and hoping that economic cooperation would offer a soft route to get to these other objectives, we now live in an era where Britain's priority has become the reverse – to, in the words of the policy outline contained in one government report in 2023, "protect, align and engage".[2] From a proactive, outward-facing policy towards China, the stance now is defensive and inward looking. The onus very much seems to be on the first of these three terms, with paranoia often standing in place of policy. The global economic crisis of 2008–09 eroded the confidence of the British and other Western countries, in the resilience of their economic systems. Since then, doubts have grown about the robustness of their political systems. For Britain, the chaos of the initial handling of the Brexit referendum in 2016 saw the opposition Labour Party almost fall apart, with dozens of members resigning in protest at the leadership of Jeremy Corbyn, before the ruling Conservative Party in 2022, despite having a large majority, saw the resignation of three successive leaders, one of whom managed to stay in power for only a matter of weeks, while another was forced to depart after most of their cabinet resigned in protest at their behaviour. The strains of the pandemic brought health systems to the brink of collapse. China itself also faced huge challenges. Protests in late 2022 at the ongoing lockdowns caused a final climbdown by the Chinese government. But the point was very simple: while the Chinese governance system was very problematic and could be criticized in a host of areas, the British one was prone to its own weaknesses, vulnerabilities and failures. The days in which one might preach to the other about their superiority were over. A harsher realism was not necessary.

In the space of only a few years, from 2015 to 2024, Britain and China have riden a diplomatic rollercoaster. Two powers with long and at times deep links and influence over each other have tried to create new frameworks, and a new paradigm, to work together – one that attempts to recognize the profoundly changed nature of their dynamics towards each other, and the world in which they operate. For all the local dissimilarities, crucially, environmental, technological and economic problems that have a global reach, and in some cases pose existential threats to the world if not managed, provide a new area of collaboration. The fact that these two powers who, even in the most difficult times in the past centuries have never stopped speaking or engaging with each other, can see largely eye to eye on climate change, the threats from AI, and on global health, offers at least a small ray of light. The irony is that never before has Britain and China agreed on such huge issues so completely. And never before have they disagreed on so many others. That is the story that this book will now unpack.

Tales from the "Golden Era"

The mission was simple. Get the cavalcade of limousines and the asso-ciated bus-loads of officials, diplomats and assistants up the road to the traditional pub and have a pint and some fish and chips. But things were never going to be that straightforward. The first problem was the road – a narrow country lane, which could barely accommodate a large car, let alone a fleet of buses. The second was the pub – a pretty but modest venue, which meant only a few people would actually get to go inside when the delegation finally arrived. The third was the demand that a few realistic-looking local punters be sprinkled around the place to make it appear vaguely natural for the photographers and journalists when they snapped their pictures.

The lead participants in this mini-drama were the then British Prime Minister David Cameron, and the visiting dignitary he was entertain-ing – supreme leader of China, Xi Jinping. It was September 2015, and the event was the first State Visit by a leader of the People's Republic to the UK for a decade. The specific location was Cameron's Oxfordshire constituency, at the Plough Inn at Cadsden, a pub he liked near one of his homes. There were other reasons to make a fuss about this event. From July 2012 to late 2013, relations between the two countries had hit a particularly rocky patch. In May 2012, Cameron had met with the exiled Tibetan religious leader, the Fourteenth Dalai Lama, despite vehe-ment protestations from Beijing. He had done so, on the pretext that the Dalai Lama was a spiritual personage, during a ceremony to confer a prize on the Tibetan at St Paul's Cathedral in London. He may also have calculated that as London would later that year host the Olympics, after the Beijing games in 2008, the Chinese would refrain from any major response. Despite best efforts to make the event as discrete as possible

– it was held in the undercroft of the cathedral, in private, away from the public – the reaction from Beijing was shrill and unrelenting. Britain, once again, had "offended and hurt the feelings of the Chinese people" (a standard form of complaint used by Chinese officials for many years before and after 1997).[1] A high-level delegation due to attend the opening of the London Olympics was called off, along with a planned separate visit by the then number two leader of the Chinese Communist Party, Wu Bangguo. Ministerial-level government visits between the two countries ceased. For almost 18 months, an icy silence reigned.

As some noted at the time, this had no visible impact on trade and investment. On the contrary, as Norway discovered when it was spurned over the Nobel Peace Prize committee's commendation to make their annual award to Liu Xiaobo in 2009, pragmatic engagement continued. Trade did not decline but remained steady. This had the unfortunate side effect of seeming to give the lie to the idea that visits by senior government figures served any practical purpose beyond keeping political links warm (although of course there is an argument that that has a positive, more complex indirect effect). The UK was isolated and embarrassed at the time when China's elite-level leadership was changing, and when the new party secretary and president, Xi Jinping, appointed in November 2012, was starting to make his mark. At the time, this leadership change was an event that was expected to only happen once in a decade. While every other Western leader was beating a track to Beijing to acquaint themselves with the new line up, the UK (and the Norwegians) was confined to home base. Only one minister managed to sneak in briefly over the 18-month period. Finally, the joke went, the many excellent diplomats at the British Embassy in Beijing were able to get on with some work, undistracted by the usual round of politicians arriving from head office making demands on their time and attention before flitting off to their next pressing issue.

Eventually in late 2013 the ice began to thaw, and David Cameron was granted a visit to Beijing and meetings with the top leaders. But the way in which this had been prepared – with an initial delegation led by the then Duke of Cambridge (now the Prince of Wales, William) and his new wife (who are relatively popular in China) – was ironic. For over a decade, the UK had been attempting to brand itself as cool, trendy, advanced and innovative. Wave after wave of government campaigns were waged from "Think UK" in the early 2000s onwards, to a "China Now" festival in Britain around the time of the Beijing Olympics in 2008. These promoted the idea of two countries being linked by creativity and adventurousness, unsaddled from the burden of history too far back in time for anyone to remember, where the present was bright, and the future brighter. How confusing therefore that it was that quintessential component of British traditionalism – a royal prince, who is second in line to the throne through ancient primogeniture rules, and part of a ruling clan that claims ancestry back to the ninth century – who was to be the plenipotential weapon by which this re-engagement was achieved. However, the gambit seemed to work.

The ambiguity of a power which was trying to be both old and new would have made sense in Beijing. After all, Chinese leaders refer to 5,000 years of history at the same time as they talk of "new" China undergoing massive reconstruction, in a landscape where increasingly a structure over a decade old is regarded as ancient. Even so, the events of 2013 made things clear. The UK was a power with a very different dynamic in its relationship with China. As noted previously, with an economy larger than the Chinese one in the years up to 1997, and far more prominent geopolitically, by 2013 Britain occupied a more diminished space. It was still a significant space. It ranked amongst the world's top economies and remained one of the most prominent diplomatic actors holding a seat on the permanent Security Council at the United Nations and other bodies. But it needed to live more by guile than ever before, it was working with a country which had a long memory (as Lee Kuan Yew, the late leader of Singapore reportedly said, China is a country that forgets nothing – and, he went on acidly, Japan one that remembers nothing!), the government of which had been refreshing and recrafting a message of national humiliation at the hands of colonists in the previous century at a time when the British Empire held sway. For the UK, some of its key assumptions and attitudes were being questioned, revised, and in many cases simply jettisoned as never before, as the country reappraised its role in the world.[2]

THE "GOLDEN ERA"

Since his appointment as Chancellor of the Exchequer after the election of the coalition government led by the Conservative Party in 2010, George Osborne had come to be regarded as the brains at the top level of the new administration, working as the seemingly more cerebral counterpoint to Cameron's smooth charm and public ease. A strategist whose ideas were key to bringing his party back to power after 13 years in opposition, he was unusual for one unexpected aspect of his past. Alone of the country's political elite of the previous 20 or so years, he had a direct personal interest in China. He had travelled there as a student in the early 1990s and come back with enough of a connection to pay close attention to UK relations with that country once he was in a position of influence. Perhaps the only figure who had occupied top positions in British politics to have a similar level of engagement and interest in China in recent decades was the former Conservative prime minister from the early 1970s Edward Heath. But most of his passion for the country came after he left power, rather than when he was in office. And much of the benefit of this to the national bilateral relations was devalued by his turbulent relations with the new leadership of Margaret Thatcher from 1975, a figure who had a far dimmer view of the People's Republic.

This fact marked Osborne out almost to the point of making him eccentric amongst his peers. Prime ministers, chancellors and most foreign secretaries, the clutch of top-level government positions in the British system, during and after the handover of Hong Kong regarded China as the domain of specialists and had cultivated a self-protective, often quite distant relationship with the place and its leaders.[3] This was in part due to the complex hangover of the Hong Kong negotiations. These had consumed much time and effort from the 1980s onwards when it became clear that the Chinese wanted full sovereignty of the island, and involved a great deal of argument and, at times, created large amounts of bad feeling and resentment. The last hurrah of empire and nostalgia pervaded the decade and a half from 1984 when the final agreement was signed off. During this time, officials and politicians in Whitehall and Beijing see-sawed between sporadic harmony, and then months, sometimes years, of dissent and disagreement over how what had been finally agreed might actually be implemented. The Tiananmen Square uprising in 1989, which saw protesting students in China's capital gunned down by the military and a major clampdown afterwards, worsened relations. A freeze on formal contact at the most senior level ensued for almost two years after this (at a working level, relations were maintained). Fears in Hong Kong that the people there were going to be abandoned to a hostile, aggressive communist regime in Beijing meant that British politicians and negotiators were in seemingly perpetual lose-lose territory. They were not going to get what they wanted from China and were seen as betraying the interests of the Hong Kongese they were meant to be defending.

Distrusted and condemned on all sides, the Hong Kong quandary dogged bilateral relations. Prime Minister John Major endured what some claimed was an unhappy visit to Beijing in 1991, the first leader of a major Western country to do so after 1989. He went there largely in order to secure a deal on constructing a new airport, something the city badly needed for its economic future, but which had to have China's agreement because its financing would mostly fall after retrocession occurred. Photos of his face during this visit were used for maximum propaganda purposes by the Communist Party leaders at the time – despite his clearly often lugubrious expression. They were still suffering from post-Tiananmen international isolation and needed any sign of contact and dialogue they could get with foreign leaders. This sort of happening was representative of the kind of distaste and discomfort UK leaders displayed when having to deal with China. His predecessor Margaret Thatcher expressed antipathy towards Deng Xiaoping's personal habits when meeting him during the signing of the Anglo–Chinese Joint Declaration on Hong Kong in 1984, apparently appalled by his way of hawking noisily into a spittoon placed by his feet during their formal meetings. According to her chief advisor on Chinese matters at the time, Sir Percy Craddock, however, she did come to have a grudging respect for the tough, uncompromising military and communist leader she had to negotiate with. Tony Blair, prime minister from 1997 to 2007, never expressed this sort of discomfort (by his time in power, Deng was already dead), but had sympathies that clearly lay westward to the United States, rather than straying east. His forays to China were sporadic – two in the decade he was in power – and stood in stark contrast to the annual delegations of German chancellors or French presidents. Jacques Chirac was in the habit of sending books of French poetry to the polyglot Jiang Zemin. Blair simply tried to educate them about the Third Way, the popular soft socialist ideology of the time. Nor were Blair's closest party associates any keener. His chancellor and successor Gordon Brown took several years to finally get on a plane and fly the ten hours from London to Beijing. In his three years as prime minister, however, he did at least visit twice. Foreign secretaries from the late Robin Cook to Margaret Beckett, Jack Straw and David Miliband were equally preoccupied and distracted by things ranging from the fallout of the 11 September 2001 terrorist attacks in America, to issues in the Middle East or Europe. In this context, they clearly did not regard visits to China as exciting, nor as particularly central to their main tasks. More importantly, they seldom showed much emotional responsiveness to the place, nor any indication that it spoke to their imaginations in a particularly compelling way, beyond that sometimes it intrigued and puzzled them. They had a workable, but complacent, attitude towards the country, and the spirit of their engagement was indicative of an inconvenient but glaring attitude they had: the People's Republic of China, despite its 1.4 billion people and its growing economy and influence, was of second-tier importance to them – marginal compared to the action in Brussels and Washington. In that sense, for once, the proclivities and preferences of the political elite reflected the country that they governed.[4]

Osborne's idea of declaring a "Golden Era" between the UK and China, therefore, when it was publicly announced during his visit to China over the summer and then on Xi's return visit in late 2015 was met with a mixture of bewilderment and mockery in much of the UK press.[5] The statement, after all, did sound somewhat corny. Even so, in view of the emotional distance and the largely tepid attitude of previous political leaders, the fact that Osborne was the first senior politician to show direct engagement and fascination with China, and to be willing to commit his own time and political capital to a relationship with it, was commendable, and something the Chinese seemed gratified and responsive to. His experience in the country might not have been extensive, but he had gathered a crucial insight that evaded his peers: China, with its ambitions to be a major world power, and to have its status restored as one of the key players in global politics in the twenty-first century was going to be an indisputable and unavoidable factor of the future. There needed to be a new framework for Britain to try to engage with and deal with this place. That in essence was what the "Golden Era" was somewhat clumsily trying to edge towards – a move away from the contentiousness and arguments of the past, and something more collaborative and consensual.

Interestingly, the Xi visit to the pub, where we began this chapter, at least in the Chinese media, seemed to hit home. The bar Xi visited became a favoured destination, albeit briefly, for subsequent tourist visitors from the People's Republic. So too did the habit of trying to drink warm beer – something that cut against the preference in China for colder continental fare. Even better was the power of seeing the avuncular looking Chinese leader sitting in a relaxed pose with his British counterpart, like they were the best of friends – which, at the time, even if somewhat briefly, they were.

The UK press's coverage of the visit was a different matter, and had an almost monolithic, static quality about it. Instead of the inevitably warm atmospherics of the Mandarin language version available back in China, which painted things in only the most relentlessly positive light, the UK press focused on human rights and problematic issues. This offered a taste of the kind of challenges that an idea like "Golden Era" was up against. Critics produced accusations that Britain was selling out to a nasty dictatorship and lacked principle in trying to get closer to it. Rosa Freedman, an academic, in an opinion piece at the time for "The Conversation" opined that "the UK's eyes are firmly on the financial benefits of a closer relationship with this repressive regime". She went on, "Make no mistake about it: that money is no less blood money than Congo's diamonds are blood diamonds. China's economic might is created by one of the most brutal regimes in the world".[6] A comparison might help better understand this issue of public attitude. In Australia, Xi addressed the federal parliament in Canberra during a visit in 2014, just a year before his trip to the UK. There he spoke about the negative image of his country from a public that was becoming increasingly uneasy and spooked by China's new found local prominence for them in their own homeland by requesting more ambition in their bilateral relations. "Our two countries should ensure that our development strategies reinforce each other's", Xi stated in an address to the Australian federal parliament, "and we should draw upon each other's strengths and build an even closer partnership of win-win cooperation".[7] By this time, there was much more immediacy for Australians, and more urgency in thinking through what China actually meant to them. Their vast northern regional neighbour had already become their largest trading partner, and one of their biggest investors, visibly present in everyday life. There was nothing unusual about Xi's vision therefore, and it was met with serious responses – albeit often critical and complex ones. In the UK where China was not a major trading partner (yet), nor a major investor, and where it was much more invisible, the challenge was very different. Australia, the United States, and other countries in the Asian region, seemed to be deciding that the tangible evidence of the emergence of a country with such a profoundly different sense of history, culture and values to their own, and one which was governed by a communist party, was likely to be disruptive and challenging and therefore carried with it a freight-load of complex emotional meaning that evaded easy categorization. But the remarkable feature in the UK, as already pointed out, was its seeming prevailing indifference to all of this and its commitment to a very simple, largely starkly two-dimensional, almost static and disengaged storyline. China was a harsh place, empire of big bucks and severe abuses and it was best to have as little to do with it as possible, simply leaving it to the specialists.

This can be illustrated by a look at the prevailing genres of UK media stories about China, some of which appeared at the time of the Xi State Visit. These broadly divide into two categories. They are either of the "shock and awe" variety – world's largest producer of electronic goods or microwave ovens, mostly from one factory for instance – or they hone in on terrifying stories of rights abuses and barbarity and show China's "otherness" and strangeness.[8] Those British politicians and businesspeople who were amongst the many groups engaged with China (these will be mapped out later) were habitually tripped up by this binary narrative that prevailed, forced to defend themselves with dealing with the place; were they there for the big bucks, and was that at the expense of the daily horror of life in this place? China in both these storylines was almost two wholly unrelated things. On the one hand, it was a place of outlandish, vast and incomprehensible statistics where individuals got lost in a sea of numbers and where if you got things right you could make a ton of money. On the other it was the domain of unconstrained cruelty where local people were crushed by the faceless machinery of the state. Of course, there were exceptions to this sort of approach – coverage in *The Financial Times,* for instance, or *The Economist* did try to convey a more complex reality. But they were a specialist subsection and for niche audiences. Mainstream media presentation of China for the mass market did not do nuance, something that became increasingly stark after 2018 for reasons we shall discuss later. And while the British have always had an inexhaustible appetite for stories that prove that all foreigners, whether continental Europeans, Americans, or from further afield, are weird and odd, the striking quality of this media presentation about China was their static nature – largely unchanged for almost three decades – and the way it indicated not a dynamic attitude that was being thought through as the situation changed, but more a doggedly settled disposition – something committed to, lazily, years before, and never fundamentally questioned.

This is not to deny that even a cursory look at the situation in China would find plenty of evidence of human rights abuses, workplace exploitation, protests and police repression. But any attempt to present this as one side of contemporary Chinese reality in a more complex context – one that recognized that while there were egregious examples of misuse of power and failure of justice over the last few decades, there were also mountains of evidence of a new, more rights-conscious middle class, and a large cohort of people who were living with more freedom and opportunity than ever before in the country's various histories – seemed doomed. Trying to explain this alternative, less straightforward story in an allotted few minutes on British broadcast media, to an audience whose knowledge of China varied hugely, and whose attention spans were often limited, (a position in which I have found myself many times over the past 25 years) proved how frustrating this state of affairs can be. Although China was a marginal actor for Britain, this focus did not matter much. As China became more extensive in its influence and impact, this concentration on just one, mostly negative, strand of the tale started to be increasingly problematic. There seemed to be a China people visited and saw, which was largely interesting and multifaceted, and the one presented to them in much mainstream media which was hell. Like or loath Osborne, no senior British politician before him had done much to try to supply a new slightly more nuanced narrative that reflected this, expending the political effort to do so.

Not that the Chinese officialdom and government was ever particularly helpful in changing perceptions about itself. As other countries had discovered, Beijing's early attempts at soft power promotion often proved counter-productive and clumsy – witness the almost universal distrust of Confucius Institutes, a network of places embedded in universities across the world and partially funded by the Chinese central government. These were ostensibly focused on teaching art and culture but were accused of promoting much more political, propagandistic fare. By 2024, there were 30 of these in Britain, with University College London, Cardiff University, and Lancaster all hosting them. Some, such as that at the School of African and Oriental Studies (SOAS) had closed.[9] They attracted almost persistent criticism, with claims that they were propagating Beijing-friendly messages, or undertaking even more sinister aims. These reached their peak in the era of Rishi Sunak as prime minister, who initially promised to close them all down in 2023, before realizing that Britain had precious little facility to learn Mandarin, and that this therefore would be a retrograde step. The measure was promptly reversed. Presumably, the calculation was that it was better to have some level of Chinese teaching in Britain, even if it sometimes carried thinly veiled propaganda, rather than have none at all and bask in complete ignorance. For all the scare stories about the potency of these places, to put things in perspective, however, in 2018, globally, there were about 525. The UK contingent was relatively small, impacting only a few thousand people who did various courses there. It is hard to see how they merited the large amount of scare stories and worries directed at them.[10]

The paradox therefore was not that China was so effective at brainwashing others, but how poorly its efforts were. For a candidate great nation and an economic superpower to expend so much effort on kicking up a fuss about Tibet, Taiwan, Tiananmen, and matters like that, put China into precisely the framework that the Chinese government's most energetic critics benefited from. The treatment of Nobel Prize winner, the late Liu Xiaobo, mentioned above, and of his wife Liu Xia, was a highly representative example. Liu Xia was held under what was in effect house arrest since 2009 until her final exile to Germany in 2018 after Liu died of cancer, despite never being formally accused or proven to have committed any crime. This was among the most poignant and upsetting examples. But, alas, there were plenty of other cases every bit as harrowing as this.

Some of them came uncomfortably close to home. The kidnap of the Hong Kong booksellers over 2015 into 2016 is a prime example. The group had been associated with small publication outfits in the special administrative region, which had specialized in issuing salacious accounts of the private lives of mainland (and sometimes local) leaders. There was nothing new about this. Such "underground" literature had thrived for decades. Their particular crime was issuing the account of someone claiming to have once been Xi's lover. The group may have assumed that Hong Kong's relative level of autonomy from the People's Republic would keep them immune from the authorities across the border. This was not to be the case. At different times, and in different ways, the five were abducted and taken to the mainland where they then separately appeared on television giving what looked like scripted confessions. Things were complicated by the fact that at least one of them was a British passport holder. More damaging still was the case of British businessman Peter Humphreys, detained and then convicted of corruption in 2014 despite his consistent statements that he was innocent and had suffered a miscarriage of justice. Humphreys was released after being diagnosed with prostate cancer in 2016. But his account of the workings of the Chinese legal system, and the real challenges he faced in getting any proper representation and protection even as a foreign national in China served as a chilling reminder that in the era of Xi Jinping, the basic assumption, if you fell foul of the authorities, of guilt over innocence was going to continue, no matter who you were, how long you had been there, or who you were working for. And while in both cases the British government did make representations, and even, in that of the booksellers, named it as a violation of the Joint Declaration and the hand-back arrangements for the region in the biannual report presented by the Foreign Office to parliament in 2016, it was also increasingly clear that the Chinese government was in no mood to take any notice of such representations. Indeed, a spokesperson for the Chinese Ministry of Foreign Affairs was to declare, when hearing of this report, that the Joint Declaration having been implemented in 1997 no longer had any meaning – something that was technically wholly wrong and which the British government promptly denounced.[11]

A Chinese government with often very inept and crude messaging techniques, which was strong on speaking about positives, and either ignored or responded defensively and with hostility on matters it regarded as more negative, was a problematic ally for a senior government minister in the UK trying to create a new kind of relationship. The Xi visit in October 2015 in its conduct and shaping was indicative of this underlying ambiguity and uneasiness – highly managed, down to the last detail, as the trip to the pub exemplified. This often involved such fierce protocol negotiations that Queen Elizabeth was caught commiserating with the police officer charged with the visit's security arrangements over the often aggressive and unreasonable demands of the Chinese while giving her an award some time after the event.[12] The pub visit had been one of the main publicity high points of the five-day tour – along with a trip to Manchester and its football clubs. But Xi and his minders stayed behind a cordon of cast iron solidity, where every moment was scripted. The onlookers in the pub were security vetted. There were no walkabouts, nor any spontaneous interaction with the British people. Beyond legitimate safety issues there always lurked the terror that someone might say something or do something that confronted or unsettled the Chinese VIP. Memories of the incident in which an irate member of the audience at a talk given by former Premier Wen Jiabao in Cambridge in 2009 threw his shoe at the dignitary (luckily, missing him) came to mind. Such things could never, ever, reoccur. The main message from the visit by anyone observing its coverage in the press was all too simple to caricature: China was a newly wealthy country; there was money to be made dealing with it; consequently British leaders were fawning over these slightly formal, stilted looking Chinese men (almost all senior Chinese leaders are men) with their famously dyed hair. This did not look like a promising platform from which to relaunch such a critical relationship and try to reach into the hearts and minds of the British public.[13]

THE "GOLDEN ERA" TURNS SILVER – THEN TO DUST

The highlight of visits by Chinese leaders, at least in modern times, is the signing with great fanfare of large amounts of trade deals and investment protocols, something that fits all too neatly into one of the strands of British media fixation with China. The 2015 Xi visit was no exception: £40 billion worth of contracts was announced.[14] The most important was the Chinese equity investment in the nuclear plant at Hinkley Point. Of a similar value, Oxford University and China Construction Bank through a subsidiary signed a £6 billion deal to help fund regenerative medicine.[15] There were also a raft of smaller agreements. These were to form the backbone of the new "Golden Era". As of 2024, most of these are, as so often with those signed with China, still to be fully realized, or, in the case of Hinkley Point, are now moribund. After much argument – the new prime minister Theresa May called the deal in to be scrutinized for a month before finally approving in 2017 – by 2023, the Chinese partner CGN halted its funding, with the British government and the French energy provider EDF stepping in.[16]

Initially, the first major turbulence to take the shine off the "Golden Era" was nothing to do with China. On 23 June 2016 in the UK, a referendum was held to decide whether the British did, or did not want to remain as members of the European Union, an organization they had joined over 40 years earlier. While Cameron had already made it clear on his re-election in 2015 that he would stand aside at the next general election scheduled for 2020, he had looked up to this point secure. Osborne figured as his most likely successor. That meant that the UK's chief patron of the "Golden Era" was likely to be politically influential well into the 2020s. The fates of these two leaders however were unexpectedly upended by the referendum result. Fifty-two per cent supported leaving. Cameron, who had staked so much on this not happening and the vote being in support of continued membership, was gone within a few weeks, fatally wounded by the result. Osborne lasted no longer: he was dismissed as Chancellor of the Exchequer by Cameron's successor, Theresa May, and left the Houses of Parliament permanently during the snap election in June 2017.

Osborne and the case of China prove that a single leader and their energy and interests in a policy area can make a big difference. Once he had gone, the "Golden Era" was immediately downgraded. May was a politician with a background largely dealing with domestic issues (she had been Home Secretary between 2010 and 2016). Until a hasty attendance at the G20 Hangzhou meeting soon after becoming prime minister, she had never even been to China. Her month-long deliberations over the Hinkley Point deal was enough to make the long-term Chinese ambassador in the UK, Liu Xiaoming, take to the newspapers at the time demanding that this unfriendly behaviour cease and the deal be allowed to proceed.[17] Even more ominous was the lines that May's closest advisor, Nick Timothy, had taken in the past, being highly critical of China's human rights record.[18] As a sign of things to come, a Conservative group of parliamentarians and activists produced a hard-hitting report on human rights, outlining the kind of worries that had been present for years before but which, during the heat of the "Golden Era", had been lost sight of.[19] Gold was apparently slowly turning to silver, and at times even looked scuffed enough to barely pass as bronze. Was the Osborne era with China really all a fantasy?

One factor that initially had to be borne in mind is the question, in the aftermath of the Brexit vote, of whether political behaviour during this period was a temporary aberration, or whether it presented something new and long lasting. We now know almost a decade later that indeed British, and international politics did start to change at this time, with the rise of populism and more nationalistic politics, far greater criticism of globalization, and the general fragmentation of the domestic political landscape. May went to the country for an election in 2017, only to lose most of her majority. For the next two years her government survived, before she was felled by an internal coup in 2019. Her successor, the populist Boris Johnson, managed to get an unexpected victory when he called an election in late 2019, but over the next three years his government was buffeted by domestic and external turbulence, and an almost continuous series of scandals about its own behaviour. Britain had once worried about the stability of the Chinese system. I remember agonized discussions about this and what the UK could do to make sure it remained unified and functional when I was an official in the early 2000s. From 2015, the situation was reversed, with the conversation being more Chinese (and others) worrying whether the UK was able to hold together. From the referendum on the future of Scotland in the Union in 2014, to the impact of Brexit and its final achievement in 2020, from the vantage point of an external observer it was Britain, not China, that looked to be the vulnerable one, and the one whose future was most at risk. This was an extraordinary reversal.

All of this meant that those realignments and structural changes where power was shifting in China's favour mentioned in Chapter 1 only accelerated after 2015. As the British economy remained stagnant, and at times contracted, China continued to grow, albeit at a slower rate, but still managing to achieve 5–6 per cent a year up to 2023. Its military continued to expand. Its geopolitical reach grew so that it managed to keep armies of think tankers and analysts outside of China in business producing ever more shrill, terrifying reports about a final takeover of the global order by this new, and in their eyes, hostile power.

Brexit made one thing crystal clear that was germane to this: in leaving the EU, for good or bad, the UK's role in the world was going to become much more complex. This was because Brexit removed one of the largest set of certainties that had been there for over four decades, namely an international trade relationship that was largely outsourced to the EU in Brussels, and a host of diplomatic positions on human rights and values which had simply existed by being aligned with the common positions across the other EU member states (something discussed in more detail later). In opting to step out of these, the UK had committed to a role in the world where it would be more autonomous and could pursue a set of new relationships according to its own interests. But it was also a world where it was more isolated. At the head of these potential targets for a new enhanced relationship was China. That, in theory, could have upgraded relations with the PRC, rather than made them more difficult and contentious.

On the very day of the 2016 referendum, ironically, a new strategic paper on EU–China relations was issued by the European Commission in Brussels.[20] Unlike the predecessor, which came out in 2006, this one was twice the length, and had lost its somewhat missionary-style language of helping China in its political, legal and social reform. In the late era of Hu Jintao (Xi Jinping's predecessor for the decade up to 2012), and into the early years of Xi, it became increasingly, and starkly, obvious that the Chinese government had no intention of adopting Western-style liberal multi-party democratic models, or setting up systems in which there were divisions of powers, and federalist, forms of governance à la the West. Xi Jinping and his co-leaders had spelt this out categorically, and consistently: there would be no such reforms. The country would find its own path, they stated, and make its own way. Just as there had been Marxism–Leninism with Chinese characteristics, then capitalism with Chinese characteristics, now democracy with Chinese characteristics was imminent. The EU 2016 document seemed to have imbibed the lessons from this new tone of politics in China and was guided by pragmatism, concentrating on specific investment, cooperation, and trade protocols rather than anything more abstract. At its heart, it demonstrated a much tougher awareness of what the EU needed to get from China, rather than what it was willing to give. On another level, too, it was also a statement of surrendering an early set of aims and ideals – an admission that engagement had not led to a China that looked more like the democratic world, but one that was resolutely bucking the modernization theory trend. This was the theory that at a certain economic point in a country's development (usually regarded as happening when it reached about $12,000–13,000 per capita income) there must be concomitant political reform – and that these have invariably involved wider participation by the middle class in decision making. Usually the assumption here is that some form of multi-party democracy has to be introduced for this to happen. Most agreed by the mid-2010s that if economic engagement with China culminating in their 2001 entry to the World Trade Organisation (WTO) was motivated by eventually seeing China adopt a political model more like the West, then this had proved a resolute failure. Even worse, under Xi the attitude seemed to be that China was better, stronger and more stable under its one-party system, and was offering a model that others might look at as an alternative to the multi-party one favoured by the United States and the EU. Against such a newly emboldened and unreconstructed partner, the EU therefore could only use the strategic advantages it had – technology, market size and wealth – to get what it wanted in the PRC: more trade, better returns on investment, and access to the hearts, minds and, most importantly of all, pockets of the great emerging middle class.

The EU since its formal establishment with the Maastricht Treaty in 1993 has presented itself as a community bound together not just by common interests and identity in terms of trade, but also by ideals and social values. The latter have become an increasing source of tension with a China which has grown ever more weary of being, as its leaders see it, lectured by outsiders. Their patience is particularly challenged when these sermons come from a group of countries which are firstly often demonstrably disunited amongst themselves despite their bold rhetoric on the surface, and secondly included some of the core players in the history of victimization and colonization that China had suffered during earlier periods of its modern history. For China, as the 2000s wore on, the EU appeared to be forever engaged in empty moralizing, lacked hard power to back up its rhetoric, and often seemed ineffective (when dealing with the initial impact of the financial crisis in 2008) and over-complicated (when trying to arrange an investment deal with Beijing – something that it promptly verified in 2019 when at least a partial deal was secured between the two and then promptly could not be ratified on Brussels side due to dissent from sanctioned Members of the European Parliament).

Whatever the larger problems, the UK was able to travel a dual route as a member of this consortium and gain some benefits for itself. Sometimes, it joined the EU pack and faced China as one of the 28 member states – particularly in negotiating trade deals, as had been the case with entry to the WTO up to 2001. In this way, it benefited from the scale of the EU and the ability to bargain from a position of relative strength. At other times, when fighting for good investment opportunities and specific trade deals conducive to its own companies that were in competition with those elsewhere in Europe, it was able to wrap itself in a Union Jack and simply badge itself as the United Kingdom. Brexit, when it happened, put an end to that dual persona, meaning the Union Jack alone rather than it and an EU flag was to be draped around Britain for good. The UK is now just the UK, geographically part of Europe, but the rest of the time floating around for better or worse in its own geopolitical universe.

In theory, this sort of liberty should have offered as decent a base as any for a golden age, a resetting of bilateral relations. The UK could, now out of the EU, sign its own bespoke free-trade deals with China. It could pursue a relentlessly bilateral and self-interested strategy, and one freed of the moralizing, more idealistic tone that the EU often adopted. It could finally be unashamed about putting itself ahead of its neighbouring European competitors when it went to China. Unleashed from the chains of Brussels bureaucracy and its inhibitions and prescriptions, the Brexiteers' argument went, the UK should have been able to create its own kind of relationship on its own terms playing to its own strengths with an emerging market like China. It could enjoy the opportunities available there as never before, many of which had been blocked off by the controlling, restrictive hand of the European Union.

This narrative conformed to the British self-image of being pragmatic and not prone to idealism or high-blown rhetoric when it came to dealing with the wider world. That fault is usually ascribed to continentals, with their preference for large abstract philosophical systems and strange federalist political habits and modes of legal thinking. Despite this, the post-Brexit vision of a new British approach to China has, over the period from 2020 to 2024, often been surprisingly idealistic and every bit as moralizing at times as the old EU style. Having left a solid, predictable relationship with the UK's largest trading and investment partners, which it had while in the EU, and departing from a free-trade deal regarded as the world's best – that of the common market and customs union the EU offered – the proposition became that a raft of more distant, less developed markets would naturally, and quickly, fill this gap. The EU, after all, still in 2024 accounts for 41 per cent of the UK's exports (with the United States and Canada taking up a large chunk of the rest), 51 per cent of its imports, and, with the US, over half of its direct inward and outward investment.[21] Cameron's replacement as prime minister in 2016, Theresa May, and her colleagues captured this idea by talking of "Global Britain". Speaking in January 2017 about her baselines for the UK exiting the EU, she stated: "I want us to be a truly Global Britain – the best friend and neighbour to our European partners, but a country that reaches beyond the borders of Europe too. A country that goes out into the world to build relationships with old friends and new allies alike."[22] For this vision of global Britain, India, Latin America, members of the Commonwealth, and, in particular, China, would suddenly have to figure in British lives as never before. UK companies would have to start to sell into a Chinese market of 1.4 billion consumers. Chinese companies would have to start to come to and be active in the UK as investors and employers in unprecedented ways. Why shouldn't this happen after all? Even before the "Golden Era", work went on to try to build a better framework at least for some forms of engagement. London has been a Chinese currency hub since the 2000s. Chinese companies like Huawei were already present in the UK from around the same time, and almost 150,000 Chinese students in 2017 were studying in the country. With a bit of focus and attention, the more zealous argued, this relationship should easily boom. That was the heady logic of the most optimistic Brexiteers.

The question of just how this all worked out in practice after the final exit in 2020 has already been referred to a number of times. Things, as ever, were much more complicated when they finally happened than originally anticipated. At the heart of this was the question of what the British might actually want even when they seemingly had greater latitude and choices. Like most simple questions, when applied to the specific case of what it wanted from China this one turned out to be fiendishly hard to offer succinct, convincing answers to.

In this whole question of what is wanted, presumably one is avoiding (as will be discussed later) the idea that on one hand it desired nothing, and on the other, everything. Neither would be realistic or reasonable. As ever, truth and reality lie somewhere in between two extremes. The simplest and most prosaic answer to the question was that the UK was largely guided by self-interest in its aims with China. That meant it wanted tangible things like capital, investment and wealth, and job-creating opportunities from Chinese partners either through them being active here, or British entities being active in China, or in partnership in other locations like Africa or elsewhere. Within this, there were opportunities the UK would be happy with, and ones on security or other grounds that it would not.

In being selective and discriminating about which of these aims to pursue, which to reject and what priorities to give them, the British will need self-knowledge, knowledge of who the UK is dealing with, and an understanding of what it actually thinks about them and their capacities and abilities to deliver. There is little point in having either over optimistic aims, or ones so pessimistic as to not be worth pursuing. In addition, there has to be recognition in this mix that because China, after all, is not just a foreign country, but differs markedly from the UK's recent principle economic and diplomatic partners, that makes things even more difficult. For most of the last century, Britain's main diplomatic alliances and relations have been in Europe and North America. These are ones it has shared cultural, linguistic, and political commonalities with, along with sharing a body of mutual knowledge, much of which, admittedly, was gained through processes of conflict, deep argument and, at times, war (perhaps the quickest and most impactful way to really learn about another partner!). China is a place with a radically different political system to Britain's today, along with a divergent set of social, religious and political values. These are marked not by a common Christian basis as in Europe or the United States, but by a complex, hybrid and often contradictory network of Buddhist, Daoist, Confucianist and now Marxist–Leninist themes. To thicken the plot even more, China also has complex relations not just with the UK, but with some of the UK's closest security allies.

The UK has a history of embracing free trade and laissez-faire capitalism, at least during some phases of its development after industrialization and the spread of globalization in the modern era. Some such as government trade minister Liam Fox argued that post-Brexit it could return to these habits, opening up almost every domestic sector to China from telecoms to critical infrastructure (two areas that are usually quite protected on security grounds) in ways that marked it out as clearly different to other European or North American economies. On the surface these sorts of decisions of who was invited to invest, on what terms, and why should be a sovereign choice. But as became even more starkly apparent from the first Trump administration's trade wars with China, what new opportunities did open up sometimes came at a cost to Britain's relations with, for instance, the United States, and others in Europe. Simply taking money and doing business heedless of these other issues was not an easy option. At times, because of the influence of third parties, the door closed completely rather than got kicked open. The final demand by the British government in 2021 that Huawei equipment be removed from 5G infrastructure in Britain for instance was done largely after pressure from the US. This sort of example proved there were opportunity costs for Britain when it was outside the EU as well as those that it felt constrained it when within. In this context, the issue soon after 2020 became not so much that the UK wanted, and would find in China, new possibilities. These almost certainly existed, though the turbulence in the Chinese economy and its own protectionist turn made these shrink to some extent. The question was more about what challenges and threats pursuing these would involve both from China, and with others. In the post-Brexit era, boundaries did not magically disappear, and the atmosphere did not become more freewheeling. Far from it. Things just became more vexed, circumscribed and complex. Ensconced within the EU the UK had a security framework and a set of shared protocols and assumptions that supplied a context within which to think about these issues of how to engage with a partner like China, and on what terms. Outside, it lost even the little predictability that provided and needed to address these issues on its own.

The associated question, not of what the UK wanted from China, but of what it might expect China wants from it, is, ironically, slightly easier to answer and will be dealt with in the following chapter. Never before has Britain had to think so carefully about what might be realistic, and what is not possible, about Chinese expectations towards it. There could be no place for naivety here. China since 1978 has thought long and hard about the West, and how to work with it, compete with it, gain benefit and advantage from it. It did this for the simple fact that over that time, it was the weaker party and the one that had to be most protective about itself. Like most Western countries over this period, the UK, while the subject of observation, has been doing very little observing back. That meant that by the time China became too prominent and important too ignore, Britain realized it had a critical lack of human capital with skills, from language to understanding of culture, to work either in China or with the Chinese coming to the UK – something that has received widespread recognition from government to politicians to business.

It is extraordinary to note that over the period from the "Golden Era" to 2022, those enrolled in British universities studying Chinese language or culture declined, rather than rose. In the UK, 850 British students were enrolled in 2014/15. This fell to 785 in 2019/20. It has since fallen further. That means that each year, on a three- or four-year course (as honours Chinese degrees usually are) no more than 260 students graduate.

While efforts have been made to teach Mandarin language at schools in Britain, so that according to the Joint Council for Qualifications (JCQ), there were 3,648 Chinese GCSE entries in the UK in 2021 and 7,091 in 2023, an increase of around 50 per cent, that has occurred against a backdrop of increased numbers of Chinese coming to British schools who often take these exams, slightly distorting the figure. This is particular the case for the high A Level, where there were 1,499 A Level Chinese entries in 2023, slightly up from 1,312 in 2021 (but still some

Table 2.1 Number of students studying Chinese at UK universities, 2014/15–2019/20

Year	Total students enrolled	From UK	From EU	Non-UK/EU
2014/15	1,440	850	190	395
2015/16	1,385	895	175	315
2016/17	1,420	925	180	315
2017/18	1,325	885	170	270
2018/19	1,225	805	160	260
2019/20	1,150	785	160	205

Source: British Association for Chinese Studies (2021: 13).

way behind the 2,272 in 2019). The A Level is notoriously difficult, and despite almost three decades of lobbying, has not been reformed from the exam offered originally largely to those of Hong Kong descent in the UK.[23]

Beyond this lack of basic linguistic skills, there is the equally important fact that, as shown in Chapter 1, the UK is dealing with a country that has a narrative towards it, but for which it has, until Osborne's "Golden Era", largely lacked an answering counter-narrative of any great sophistication. These are all sources of potential vulnerability and weakness. Someone with a plan towards you is likely to be in a stronger position, as long as that plan is realistic and evidence based, than someone with no plan at all who leaves everything to chance. Sporadic opportunism and letting things take their "natural course" may once have been fine, when the amount and level of engagement was modest and the costs of failure and mistakes relatively low. With China and the UK, however, if there are ever to be increases in the areas of trade and diplomatic engagement, this must mean that the more casual, laissez-faire attitude is no longer fit for purpose, and the price of getting things wrong has increased dramatically. That is something that the heightened anxiety and fear of a stronger, more strategically focused China which rose sharply from 2020 onwards made clear. Britain is often posited as a pragmatic actor, one which dislikes over-structured diplomatic strategies because of the ways these impede flexibility and the ability to respond to new situations in new ways. But with China, because of the speed of change, and the risks and areas of potential disagreement or conflict if things go wrong, a plan of engagement (or, at times, non-engagement) is necessary, however loose and flexible. To do this, the UK needs to work out clearly what kind of entity it thinks it is dealing with in China, and where the real risks and opportunities are.

This book will assume therefore that a strategy of some sort is a necessity, not an optional add on. The 2021 and 2023 Integrated Review after all, on a global scale, argues that this is something Britain needs for all its relationships, not just those with China. What sort of shape that strategy might take will be addressed in the rest of the book, and whether these reviews actually fit the bill. Alongside this will be the related question of what corresponding attitude needs to be adopted to make this strategy viable or work. But to start, to orientate ourselves better, let us turn to the question of what China wants from the UK.

What does China want from the UK?

What does China want? This was a commonly asked question by businesspeople, politicians and commentators not just in the UK, but throughout the world as they engaged with this newly emerging power through the 2000s and into the 2010s. Throughout Asia, North America, Central Asia, the Middle East, and into Eastern, Central, and finally Western Europe and the rest of the world, figuring out China's plans and desires towards itself and the international community were of central concern. Interpreting these desires correctly, working out how to leverage them or gain benefits from them, and whether to see them as benign or more assertive and threatening, became the work of diplomats, businesspeople, analysts and politicians the world over.

By the end of 2020 it seemed the world had reached its conclusion. China, whatever the specifics of what it wanted, was after things that were antagonistic, threatening and against the interests of the political West. It was a threat, at times described as existential in its depth. As already noted, British politicians sometimes started to echo this language. From 2020 to 2024 many indulged in the luxury of pretending there was a global future where China could be painted into the corner and shouted at or shamed into compliance. Whatever interpretation of this period we might wish to adopt, one thing is clear. It marked a watershed. Even the most complacent and parochial could no longer regard China as marginal and insignificant. The question of what it was, and what it wanted, became not less but more urgent.

The Chinese government's statements about its own plans and desires are not unproblematic and often do not help much in working out its intentions, as the previous chapter recognized. Under Hu Jintao an increasingly heavy silence reigned. The most the world got were

statements of "peaceful rise" and "harmonious co-operation". Such sop-
orific rhetoric was hard to work with, particularly as China's actions
– aggression in the South and East China Sea, and shrill declarations
of hurt feelings when criticized over matters like Taiwan, Xinjiang or
Tibet, which it considered domestic ones – often seemed completely
at odds with its muted language when addressing international relations. Demands in the United States and elsewhere that China made a
clearer statement of its intentions became unavoidable when confronted
with the burgeoning size of the country's economy. From 2002 to 2012,
despite the negative impact of the world financial crisis in 2008, China
quadrupled its GDP from $1.4 trillion to $8.5 trillion.[1] Other economies
like that of the United States managed less than double that growth.
China could no longer hide its size and significance on the world stage,
even if it wanted to.

With Xi Jinping, from 2012, there was a major corrective. In his first
five years in office, he asked his fellow politburo members to tell the China
story. He also asked his diplomats to be proactive. The Belt and Road

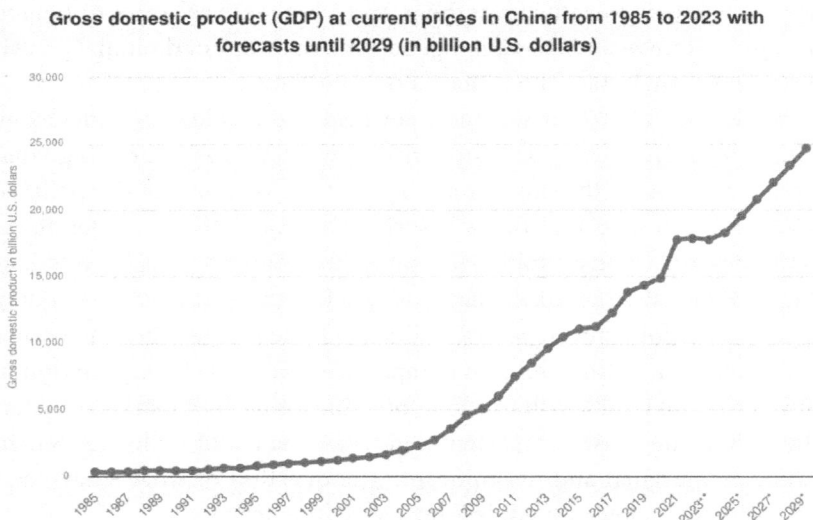

Figure 3.1 China gross national product, 1985–2029 (projected).

Source: Statistica, https://www.statista.com/statistics/263770/gross-domestic-
product-gdp-of-china/

Initiative was amongst the most important of these new statements of intent: the grand geopolitical idea first articulated by Xi in 2013 as "The New Silk Road" and attempting to map out a Chinese vision of how it engages with the world around it on balanced, mutually beneficial ways. At its heart were a number of clear messages. First, China wanted to be a different kind of power from the United States, rather than competing with it, but it did want equality of status. Secondly, it was willing to use its greatest asset – the size of its economy and the growth potential in services and other emerging sectors – as an inducement for others to increase their engagement with it and link with it more deeply. Thirdly, it had more than just an economic vision: it wanted an Asian region around it driven by what it called common destiny and a world of multipolarity, where its values were at least accommodated and better understood by others. Finally, in practical terms it wanted connectivity, through improved infrastructure, finance, communications, people-to-people links and technology, to create integrated markets, logistics routes, and something like a global community with Chinese characteristics. There was one thing it evidently did not want: an American-style hegemony, where it would one day figure as the global police and peacemaker, distracted and burdened by the security needs of others, and having to foot the bill for them. In essence, these were the things China under Xi said it wanted.

Later, as the country moved into the more turbulent period after Trump's first election, and the pandemic, there was a modification of this more purely internationalist vision. From around 2020 it made clear that it wanted a partial decoupling and greater autonomy in terms of technology and control over critical parts of its domestic economy. The notion that became popular amongst Chinese leaders from 2021 was "dual circulation". That supplemented the idea a few years earlier of "Made in China 2025" – creating a country which was no longer in technology deficit with the outside world, but had world-class research and development capabilities, and was not beholden to the West to supply its intellectual property. "Dual circulation" accepted that a total casting off links with the outside world was not remotely an option. Xi Jinping is not an isolationist. But he was certainly increasingly a nationalist, seeking to make China great again, bolstered by the ideology produced by his key thinker, Wang Huning, to make a country with cultural confidence, proud to be itself and look the outside world in the eye as a complete equal.

One of the starting points for addressing these strategic questions for the UK approach to China is how it might work with this world view, and in what ways it might benefit, modify or need to oppose this view. As Chapter 1 made clear, in the era up to the return of Hong Kong to the Chinese, the UK was a significant partner that was larger economically than China. Since then, the story is one of rapidly shifting influence in China's favour, across almost all areas. As part of the EU, the UK still figured as a significant, and core member, of the world's largest and wealthiest market. Outside of the EU, once it managed to finally leave in early 2020, the UK's appeal became diluted. In contrast, most nations of the world in the period up to 2020 seemed to want a part of the great emerging opportunity that was China, especially as the country appeared to become ever more ambitious and inclusive. Almost in every part of the world over this period there were conferences and seminars on the Belt and Road Initiative, and investment delegations travelling to and fro. Political and business leaders vied for China's attention. Xi Jinping, in the five years after becoming leader, was a guest in almost 50 countries. In each one, he was feted like visiting royalty. *The Economist*'s cover story in October 2017 stated what most people were coming to suspect – that the world's most powerful man sat not in Washington but in Beijing.[2]

In some ways, the UK's more sceptical attitude towards China, particularly post-Brexit, was a step ahead of the rest of the world. It was pro-engagement, with the slight blip of the "Golden Era" trying to warm things a little, but no desire for a full-blown elopement with the great power the other side of the world. When the harder times came, therefore, from the Trump trade wars of 2018 onwards, Britain was, in terms of its disposition towards China, well placed. Through its complex experience with the country, it was able to see through much of the hyperbole. The problem was that it found itself, for reasons entirely unconnected with China, in a position where, adrift from the EU, it needed to forge a global role again for itself as a more unilateral actor. That meant working out how to engage with a place that in 2020 constituted a fifth of the world's GDP.

The UK faced the formidable task of seeking an upgraded and more intense relationship at a time when it had never appeared more marginal

and smaller. This is not to belittle the UK – it is still a significant economy, and a major military and diplomatic player in 2025, even after the
turbulence of the post-Brexit years – but its current capacities are a
long way from those that existed in the not-so-distant past, and have
been shown to be even more vulnerable against a China that has never,
in modern history, been stronger. The disparity has been increasing in
both directions and widens daily. Even in the final quarter of 2024, as
the Chinese economy struggled to achieve 5 per cent growth, the UK
achieved two terms of zero increase in GDP.

Given this context, therefore, does China want anything from the
UK? Is the UK, now outside the far larger trading entity of the EU, so
remote and increasingly unimportant that it does not figure in Chinese
leaders' thinking at all? Xi's visit in 2015, and that of his then premier
the late Li Keqiang in 2014, made clear that Britain did still matter over
this period. These were lengthy, high-profile visits. From them, and from
what Chinese leaders said, it was clear they still factored the UK into
their thinking. Within the grand international narratives they promoted,
the core things about the UK that mattered and continue to matter to
them become clear, as one looks at the record over the decade of change
and transformation for everyone from 2015.

The Chinese interests in the UK in 2015 fell into three broad categories: investment, finance and intellectual partnership (the latter inclusive
of technology and expertise). To some extent, these things still matter
a decade later in 2025. But the deteriorating political and geopolitical situation, with far greater antagonism and distrust on both sides,
means that they are now located in a very different context with much
more complexity factored in than before. One of the main changes is
that across the board, securitization has intensified. For China, with its
various national security laws and regulations restricting the work and
access of foreigners in China, it has become a far less open economy
than before. But Britain has more than reciprocated. Its own National
Security Act passed in July 2023, according to the press statement
released to announce it, for the first time made it an offence "to be an
undeclared foreign spy materially assisting the activities of a foreign
intelligence service in the UK".[3] Plans to ask people to maintain a register
of contacts with citizens from countries of concern (and that invariably
included China) were also discussed, although at the time of writing has

not yet passed. Through a combination of accumulated distrust, and the general overall environment internationally, Britain and China despite their very different political systems and outlooks, became a little like mirror images of each other. Their posture was more defensive and the calculation of risk far higher.

Despite this, the three areas listed above are still important. In some ways, as the UK hits even more severe challenges as it searches to deal with its economic issues from low productivity to sluggish growth and increased barriers to the EU market these have become even more urgent. China remains the most challenging opportunity cost. It places increased restrictions and stipulations on those wanting to engage with it, and yet, for a power like the UK, not engaging carries a high economic and geopolitical price.

INVESTMENT

The UK has long presented itself as an open and liberal investment environment. According to the World Bank, Britain in 2020 ranked eighth in terms of "ease of doing business".[4] China came in well down that list at thirty-first.[5] In 2023–24, Britain came second in Europe, in terms of attractiveness as a destination of foreign direct investment (FDI).[6] In 2023, Britain ranked third in terms of stocks of inward FDI after the US and China.[7] As a mature, open, liberal, rules-based, predictable, transparent investment destination, the UK was, and remains, highly competitive. This is testified to by the high number of acquisitions by American, Japanese and European companies in the period from 2010. There are fewer restrictions over sectors available for investment in the UK by non-British parties, and more diverse opportunities for majority or complete ownership. UK corporate tax rates (25 per cent in 2025) are relatively competitive amongst developed economies, and the rule of law is respected and regarded as reliable. Corruption levels are low, and rates of return, while not comparable to those of some emerging economies, healthy and, at least in recent history, steady.

Since the late 1990s, China has become an increasingly active outward investor. It barely ranked as a deployer of capital and acquirer of companies and assets outside its own border before this. Indeed, in the

Maoist era (1949–76), this kind of engagement with the capitalist West would have been regarded as anathema. But a combination of needs for markets, aftersales support for its exports, technology and know-how, brands, and, above all, resources, meant that from the 1980s, slowly, Chinese FDI increased. At the same time as it was absorbing a huge amount of foreign capital, it was also starting to buy mining companies, energy interests, and a miscellaneous group of other companies abroad. In the late 1990s, Chinese investment in the UK was a novelty. There were a few large names – for example, the Bank of China and PetroChina – but hardly enough to merit much interest. On the whole, British government delegations at this time tended to focus on countries wth existing investment links – Japan, South Korea, and the United States. Even India, because of a significant ethnic population in the UK, ranked more highly than China.

Having joined the WTO in 2001, the Great Financial Crisis of 2007–08 offered China opportunities for cheap acquisitions; Beijing now had the will and wherewithal to become more engaged. Its global stocks of FDI rose. In the UK, the state-owned China Development Bank bought a small share of the British banking firm Barclays Plc. Through the management of its vast foreign currency reserves, China's State Administration of Foreign Exchange (SAFE) also acquired modest stocks in over a hundred British listed companies, including the supermarket chain Tesco and the oil and gas supermajor BP. The expectation that suddenly the UK would be flooded by Chinese money, however, proved precipitous. Although Chinese companies did come to list on the main stock exchange in London, and its smaller counterpart, the Alternative Investment Market (AIM), regulatory compliance demands and governance meant many of these had a torrid time. By 2010, the breathless expectation that China would be an investor competing with the United States and others proved wrong. It was cautious, and its investments, while increasing, remained relatively restrained. They were largely through state-owned companies, mostly through Beijing, and restricted predominantly to sectors where China had direct strategic interests: energy companies, technology-seeking companies, or those which helped it gain expertise and brands. Experience of making commitments that then turned out to be very risky, or offered political pushback or poor returns, meant the earlier appetite had been dampened.

The UK's investment figures from China, compared to the rest of the EU, have been sound but not spectacular. Chinese buyers bought brands like Weetabix, Thames Water, and even earlier on, the car maker MG Rover. They came to own the Pizza Express chain of restaurants, and had large stakes in the department store group House of Fraser, before these were divested in mid-2018 due to imminent bankruptcy. Investment figures however showed a pattern similar to other developed economies. The bulk of sectoral investment in the UK was for rent and lease or real estate. In effect, Chinese were coming to Britain to own offices to provide aftersales service for their exports, or to buy property, particularly in London, as a relatively easy way for individuals to invest. Many of the latter sales were to wealthy Chinese families who bought accommodation for their children while they studied in the UK. In terms of one of the key aims of FDI – job creation – things were underwhelming. There were no major manufacturing investments along the lines of Nissan or Honda, employing thousands in factories in less affluent parts of the UK. Instead, a company like Huawei, the telecoms giant from Shenzhen, southern China, employed no more than a thousand people in the UK by 2017. Job creation, according to early research, was not a natural outcome of Chinese FDI. By 2024, China accounted for a miniscule 0.2 per cent of total UK inward FDI stock. And for Britain, China only accounted for 0.6 per cent of its outward stock. To give some sense of comparison, for these two figures, for the United States respectively, the amount was 34 per cent and 26 per cent.[8]

The attraction of Britain for Chinese investment had initially been twofold. First, for a company like Huawei or Alibaba, Britain was noticeably more tolerant. In the United States, despite spending over $20 million in lobbying up to 2016, Huawei had been effectively blocked from most government procurement projects. In Australia in 2012, it had been banned from bidding to supply national broadband coverage. Both of these refusals were on national security grounds. Despite frequent protestations from the owners, Huawei was regarded by Washington and Canberra as a company with deep links to the Chinese state, and therefore as good as a state company. It was accused of undertaking espionage. The UK was not immune to these kinds of worries. Even as early as 2009 the UK press reported major security concerns about allowing Huawei to operate to any scale in Britain. Despite this, the company secured one of its largest projects in a mature market, supplying equipment to British Telecom. It also set up a joint centre in Cheltenham, the southwestern town where the government's signals intelligence headquarters is based, so that its codes and technology could be vetted by experts for potential abuse before being deployed. Huawei in 2018 had the headquarters of its European operations in Britain, and a board made up of eminent figures like Lord Browne, the former head of BP. Secondly, until Brexit became a reality, the UK (as Huawei illustrates, alongside another major technology company also headquartered in Britain, Alibaba) had been able to market itself as a stepping stone not just to the domestic market, but to the rest of the EU and its 400 million consumers and indeed, the whole of Europe outside the EU.[9]

After 2015, the message communicated to Beijing during the "Golden Era" was that the UK was open and more accessible to investments than any other similar economy. The quest by the UK has been to diversify this investment. Potential Chinese involvement in building or funding infrastructure like the planned second high-speed rail line (HS2) running north from London to Birmingham and beyond was mooted. Chinese capital has gone via the Chinese Investment Corporation into Heathrow, amounting to 10 per cent ownership. Most important of all at this time was the earlier mentioned equity investment in Hinkley Point nuclear power station in the Southwest of England. For HS2 and nuclear projects, China has more than simple profit in mind. It had developed technology that it now wanted to utilize in the rest of the world. Succeeding in building a nuclear plant, or a trainline, with indigenous Chinese technology in such a highly regulated environment was regarded as one of the best advertisements for its wares.

Huawei's involvement and commitment to the UK was knocked back in October 2022 when the British government, after significant pressure from the United States and others, issued a notice stating that British telecom operators needed to ensure that all the Chinese company's equipment and components was removed from 5G by the end of 2027. Although, since 2017, Huawei had set up a number of R&D centres in Cambridge, Ipswich, Edinburgh, Bristol and London employing about 250 people, its operations in Britain were extremely modest. Its main global markets were in China, Africa, Latin America and the Middle East. In some ways, as a sign of the times, by 2024, the Chinese electric car manufacturer BYD had become more viable as a flagship Chinese investment in Britain, with about 200 employees at their Uxbridge office, selling EVs into the UK market. But even here, security concerns reared their head, with the US and Europe both regarding Britain as too liberal towards the massive and hugely successful Chinese company. It would be able, they claimed, to stop cars operating if a conflict broke out, creating traffic gridlock and civil unrest.

The potential for Chinese to increase investment in Britain was not a chimera in view of Britain's relatively strong performance in attracting inward FDI and its aim to be a platform both for domestic and continental European business. But by 2024, the landscape was far less rosy than a decade before. Security concerns had become a greater priority. Reports of Chinese intellectual property theft were the norm. The British deputy prime minister in 2023, Oliver Dowden, declared that China was Britain's "chief economic threat" – almost the polar opposite of what had been the British government's position a decade before.[10] A National Security and Investment Act came into force in January 2022. This reportedly gave "the government powers to scrutinise and intervene in business transactions, such as takeovers, to protect national security, while providing businesses and investors with the certainty and transparency they need to do business in the UK".[11] In early 2024, the British government in the final days of the Conservative administration stated to the US that it would put in place greater scrutiny and demand more transparency from Chinese investments.[12] One example of this was the blocking of a Chinese company's attempts to acquire a microchip plant based in Newport, Wales, in 2022.

Brexit also complicated the picture. As with other major foreign companies, Chinese UK investors from 2020 needed to make a strategic decision about just how easy access into Europe was now that Britain had exited the EU. Because of the sheer number of other issues, however, it is hard to isolate Brexit alone to quantify what if any impact it has had so far on China's role in Britain. Chinese investments have certainly declined – but that is as much to do with geopolitical issues, the influence of the US, the securitization of the UK's general approach to China, and rising fears amongst the government about Chinese influence in Britain. Brexit is only part of this mix, and perhaps not the most significant part.

Chinese investment in the UK has paradoxically gone from being low volume and low profile in the mid-2010s, arousing little of the emotional responses that it frequently stirred up in the United States or Australia at this time – to even lower volumes and yet higher profile. It seems the less Chinese investment there is in the UK, the more the British have taken to complaining and finding issues with it. While in 2018, there was some level of interest and excitement about the possibilities of more engagement with Chinese companies, these have now soured. Surveys show a generally negative view of China and the costs of economic engagement. Under the Labour Party in government from July 2024 there was some attempt at a reset. But where once people were willing to give China the benefit of the doubt, by then the default was to assume guilt before then trying to establish if a more benign interpretation is more in order. The Chinese may be the largest and fastest builders of high-speed railways, and of nuclear power stations in the world, and they may be producing more and more high-tech products, but with the exception of EVs, Britain has been reluctant to pursue any of these with much passion or commitment. Its own second high-speed rail-line remains mired in controversy, greatly scaled back, with vast overruns in terms of cost, and an end date around 2029–33. Remembering that China built close to 47,000 kilometres of track where trains can exceed 350 kph in the decade and a half from 2008 to 2023, it is a sobering comparison of capacity and ambition. Granted, China does not face the same legislative and approval processes, which in the UK can be hugely protracted. Even so, the difference between the 100 kph high-speed track for Britain and that which exists for China is humbling. As of 2025, Britain's attitude towards Chinese investment is a bit like a starving person trying to pretend they don't feel hungry. This looks likely to change only gradually, if at all. At the same time, however, Chinese companies, state and non-state, continue to invest and involve themselves in the Global South, being one of the main players in those countries, and showing that it is these places that now most attract its interest rather than the UK.

FINANCE

The City of London is one of the world's foremost financial centres. In 2024, Z/Yen's Global Finance Centre Index announced that London was second only to New York as the world's premier finance hub.[13] In terms of business environment, financial sector development, infrastructure, human capital and reputational and living style factors, London beat Hong Kong and Singapore. In terms of market capitalization, the London Stock Exchange main market was $4.4 trillion in 2024 – the world's ninth largest.[14] It is home to one of the world's oldest and largest insurance markets, equity sales markets and banking centres.

There was much about London's prowess as a financial centre that attracted China over the 2000s into the 2010s. The fact that, unlike New York, it was only seven to eight hours behind, rather than a much less convenient 15 hours, meant that at least the end of the working day in Beijing or Shanghai could catch the start of business in London. Unlike Hong Kong, Sydney or Singapore, London was larger. It was, in 2018, the largest finance centre in Europe – and the most international in terms of companies, workforce and culture. Unlike New York at this time, it was less plagued by political issues regarding China. London was well regulated, stable and innovative.

For these reasons, the City of London Corporation which governs the financial district (the "Square Mile"), was energetic in marketing itself in the People's Republic since the late 1990s. Delegations led by the Lord Mayor (the City's main municipal representative, as opposed to the Mayor of London, who is the political leader of the whole city) started to make their way to Beijing, Shanghai and other major cities to do roadshows. In the heady days of the 2000s, as the Chinese economy boomed, companies were signed up to be listed on the London Stock Exchange (LSE). Others were encouraged to set up offices in the City, including the Industrial and Commercial Bank of China (ICBC), the Agricultural Bank of China, China Merchants Bank (the country's sole major non-state-owned banking institution), and China Construction Bank (the Bank of China opened its very first overseas branch in London in 1929). This was in addition to the Chinese Investment Corporation (CIC), the entity which was in effect the sovereign wealth fund for Beijing. China's insurance companies, and other finance providers, also started to have a presence. For most, their interest was in serving the growing number of Chinese companies coming to seek opportunities in the UK. But some also acquired British clients.

As with FDI, however, the story is one of stagnation or regression after 2017. After an initial spurt of listings on the main LSE market up to 2006, there were still only five Chinese companies as of 2020. Shein, a Singapore-based fashion firm but with extensive interests in China, was moving towards a listing by 2025 but had yet to finalize this decision at the time of writing. On the Alternative Investment Market, too, after a great deal of activity around 2006, issues about filing results, transparency about company ownership and governance, and accounting procedures meant that listed firms remained at about 36, with several subsequently delisting. While companies from the PRC looked to Hong Kong or the New York market, London has become less compelling.

London had a much more tangible and important function than only being home to banks for the Chinese government, and that was the role it could take in the process of internationalizing China's currency, the Renminbi (RMB). Historically, RMB has been a nonconvertible currency and not openly traded. This gave the government in Beijing a level of control that a more exposed currency could not have. During the Asian financial crisis in 1998, therefore, the Chinese were able to see off the worst effects of the turmoil going on around them because to some degree they were insulated from it. The same applied in 2008 during the global crisis. Over the decade from 2008, incremental moves were made to open up the Chinese capital account, but doing so in ways which tried to ensure that this did not involve risks and loss of control. Currency trading deals were signed with a number of global centres, from Sydney to Singapore, Frankfurt and Vancouver. The deal with London, however, was the most significant, allowing invoicing to be undertaken directly in RMB (thus saving on currency transaction costs when doing business with Chinese partners) and the trading of so-called "dim-sum bonds" – stocks in Chinese RMB rather than sterling.

The flow of RMB through London increased dramatically during the enthusiasm of the "Golden Era", in 2016 overtaking Hong Kong as the world's largest centre for Chinese currency trading. However, even though it was the sixth most traded foreign currency, it still only amounted to a meagre 1 per cent of global flows of traded exchange, dwarfed by the US dollar, the euro, and even British sterling. The Chinese government had made it clear, through their then head of the People's Bank of China, Zhou Xiaochuan in 2009, that they regarded the dominance of the US dollar in international business and trade as the source of immense imbalance and unfair advantage for America. But, as in the domain of geopolitics, while clear about what they did not want, there was less clarity about what they actually wanted. China did not wish its own currency to be exposed to the vagaries and uncertainties of the global market as the US dollar often was. They regarded control of the national current account as a source of strength, not weakness. But the more embedded they became within the global economy, the more this great wall of currency control between China domestically and the outside world became prominent and problematic. This was especially the case as, through the city of Shanghai, China endeavoured to construct a local finance sector for its rising middle class. For this, there needed to be more connectivity – something that was also stressed as a key part of the Belt and Road Initiative (BRI). Unsurprisingly, Shanghai, Shenzhen and then Hong Kong all outranked London by 2024 in terms of market capitalization of the listed companies.[15]

Looking at the map of those global centres that had signed currency swaps with China up to 2016, the most prominent feature was not so much who was there, but how one major player was missing – that of the world's largest economy, the United States. This was duplicated in the structure of the Asia Infrastructure Investment Bank (AIIB) and the BRI. China seemed to be constructing a world in which America was absent. It was only in 2017 that a currency arrangement was agreed with New York. Even so, the strategic role of London, as a hub of capitalism in Europe and an English-speaking environment that was not the USA, was compelling for Chinese policy-makers as they pondered how to open up their currency more to the outside world, while maintaining some level of control over the process. London has everything going for it in this emerging plan – size, diversity, location, language and governance.

By 2023, London ranked the second largest offshore RMB payments centre globally, with £120 billion trading each day, a 13 per cent increase over the previous year. Cross border settlement between Britain and China using RMB had increased to 3 trillion RMB by the end of 2023.

There were separate programmes investing in the Chinese domestic bond market for foreigners, and the increase of carbon trading.[16] This was one of the areas of relative success and stability. Even so, Beijing's attitude has become cautious with a lot of controls continuing over flows of money in and out of the country. The simple fact is that China runs a system of capitalism with Chinese characteristics. Its leaders regard the market as a political tool to sustain one-party rule. There are deep differences therefore in the conceptual world that finance in London and financiers in China work in. Will London be the great crucible in which, from these two different realms, a new hybrid, sustainable entity will emerge? That is still a possibility, in 2024, even as other areas have become more restricted, and tightened.

TECHNOLOGY AND INTELLECTUAL PARTNERSHIP

From the time of the Macartney mission to China in the 1790s, it was not capital and goods that Imperial China and its successors wanted, so much as ideas. As the economic historian, Kent Deng has written: "In hindsight, instead of British commodities, if Earl George Macartney had in 1792 offered the Qing Emperor new European knowledge represented by Isaac Newton, Gottfried Wilhelm Leibniz, Adam Smith, Thomas Robert Malthus, and so forth his embassy to China would have fared much better. So far, from what is available regarding the attitude of the Qing elite, such new European knowledge would have been well received."[17] Conceptualizing China as more than just a source of capital and as a huge potential market to sell into and make profit from in the era of its enrichment has proved difficult. And yet it was in ideas that the deficit with the outside world was most frankly and frequently admitted in the discourse of elite leaders in Beijing in the early decades of the twenty-first century. In his epic three hour and 23-minute speech at the Nineteenth Party Congress in October 2017, Xi Jinping paraded China's immense achievements under reform and opening up since 1978. He fed on the rising atmosphere of expectation and excitement as China grew closer to realizing the "Centenary Goal" in 2021: the creation of a middle-income country, with per capita GDP of around $13,000. Bourgeois China was imminent, he seemed to be saying. For the first time ever, more Chinese live in cities than in rural areas. At that time, there were 2,500 universities, with over 7 million students. In 2016, 340,000 Chinese were studying in the United States, 260,000 in Australia, and 150,000 in the UK. Never before, in such a short space of time, can the young future elites of a single country have gone abroad in such numbers for their education. And unlike in the past, many were now returning, to take up positions in business and government. One of the most prominent was Chen Jining, Mayor of Beijing from 2017 to 2022, and then Party Secretary of Shanghai from 2022 onwards. Chen was educated in the UK at Brunel University and then Imperial College, London, completing a doctorate in civil engineering there before working for a few years up to 1998 as a researcher. He now sits on his country's Politburo, currently the highest ranked figure to have such a strong British background.

Success in innovation is hard to measure. But in no area has the change been more startling and paradigm breaking than the appearance of a China that no longer imitates but tangibly innovates. British confidence was relatively high in terms of its prowess in this area in the early 2000s, promoting itself as the home to highly creative companies and research institutes. According to one statistic in 2014, that measured the amount Chinese patents make from foreign revenues, China was still a minnow. The United States managed to raise $84 billion from licensing its proprietorial technology at that time. The UK brought in almost half as much. But China accrued just a billion. The conclusion was simple. In terms of producing know-how and methods that others wish to buy on the international marketplace, Chinese efforts barely registered.[18]

By 2024, however, the situation is radically different, and more complicated. According to a number of ranking systems, in the two decades since 2005, Chinese universities have risen steadily, so that they now stand behind only the US in terms of overall representation. The Academic Ranking of World Universities listing even claims that Chinese institutions actually stood top. At a time when the rankings of most British universities were under increasing pressure, Peking, Tsinghua and Fudan continued their climb into the top 250, and then, in some cases, into the top 20.[19] Generous government research funding was one reason for this, along with the impact of the many returnees from the US and elsewhere, mentioned earlier, who had found the environment abroad increasingly hostile to academics originally from the People's Republic.

In terms of research output, too, there was dramatic change. By 2023, authors from China accounted for a quarter of the global output of published articles, reviews and conference papers, followed by 12 per cent from the USA, and only 3 per cent from the UK.[20] In 2024 China ranked top of the database of citable research papers classified by Scopus, with well over three times the number of authors based in the UK. Similarly, China has the highest share of articles published in scientific journals according to the Nature Index.[21] From areas like AI to stem cell research, life sciences, and environmental technology, China was a world leader, either at parity with Britain, or ahead of it. As for the application of this research, in 2023 the data for patents applied for and then granted for new inventions indicated that China stood top of the list, with over double the nearest competitor, the US. The UK was not even in the top ten.[22]

The rise of China as a research innovator has occurred at the same time as the UK has slipped down many international performance league tables. When it comes to funding and access to European and other sources of grants, British universities by the end of 2024 appeared buffeted and exposed, subject to financial and political pressures as never before. While Oxford, Cambridge, and then a cluster of London-based institutes like Imperial, UCL, and King's maintained global competitiveness, in terms of research outputs, they were increasingly fighting against a host of new entrants, not all from China, but with Chinese ones taking the lead. The impact of Brexit in particular was acute here, with a fall initially in the number of students from Europe as full international rate fees were asked of them rather than local ones after 2020.

British universities still do matter to China. Many still have research partnerships with Chinese entities. But these are exposed to levels of scrutiny as never before. British politicians like former leader of the Conservative Party, Iain Duncan Smith, declared in 2024 that due to the 150,000 Chinese students in Britain, universities were "in hock" with the ruling Communist Party in the PRC and that they did not dare to offend it.[23] It is easy to find increasingly shrill (and, to Chinese students, deeply unfair) claims along these lines, ranging from accusations that the Chinese Students and Scholars Association in the UK was an extension of the United Front Department from the Chinese central government, and existed to pressurize Chinese students to the notion that in classes, Chinese students were frightened to express opinions on sensitive political matters about their home country for fear of being reported. At the time of the Covid-19 pandemic, students of Chinese and Asian heritage more generally stated that there was a rise in harassment and racial abuse in the UK.[24] To complicate matters, even those seeking to study China came in for levels of attention and complaint, almost reminiscent of the McCarthyism of 1950s' America, with accusations that any contact with China and Chinese organizations was problematic. Two researchers, one who worked for the China Research Group, were charged with espionage in 2024. Their cases are ongoing.

A more measured approach was proposed by former Minister of State for Universities, Science, Research and Innovation, Jo Johnson, whose report for the King's College London Policy Institute, "The China Question" set out the quandary well.[25] For all the fears about the risks of working with Chinese entities, for British universities their revenue from students from the PRC was not so easily offset by increasing numbers coming from India, Nigeria or other markets. Despite attempts to source from these places, the Chinese cohort remained critically important. In addition, as his report made clear, intellectual engagement between the two countries had increased, rather than diminished. The exchange was not just financial now, but involved knowledge, with a transaction in ideas as well as in money. As the report stated, UK collaboration with China increased from less than 100 co-authored papers in 1990, to 16,267 papers in 2019. This amounted to 11 per cent of total UK output.[26]

The general advancement of Chinese research and development capacity and achievements, along with the increased financial precarity and diminished global rankings of British universities, serves as a powerful symbol of a relationship that has become more vexed and more challenging, but in which the UK has to face sharp opportunity costs. Britain's pre-eminence in this area of innovative research was once assumed as a given. It is now undergoing significant change. Where once China wanted closer collaboration with Britain in this area and made this one of the pillars of its relationship, signing major research deals with Oxford University when Xi Jinping visited in 2015, the tables have to some extent turned. The purists demand that all contact with

China cease because they regard it as a security threat attempting to infiltrate tertiary education and undermine British values. The realists acknowledge that such an approach would be self-harming, and probably impossible, and that there are better and more proportionate ways to deal with this challenge. Chinese innovations in AI and environmental science are becoming world leading. Cutting the UK off from access to the benefits of these would mean degrading its competitiveness and its international standing. The harsh new reality was that, in ways never so clear before, China could live quite well without the UK, but the UK would struggle without China. No field shows this more clearly than education, research and development.

CHINA'S WANTS

Investment, finance, and innovation and research are broadly the things that China had wanted from the UK, and these sat within its wider strategic ambitions in the early decades of the twenty-first century to be a great, modern, powerful nation. For each of them, the aims and aspirations outlined in the "Golden Era" have since been downgraded and become more complicated. For investment, the amount of stocks from China has remained flat and stagnated. The UK's changing views on security and foreign investment has meant the setting up of a new legislative framework where risk is viewed far more keenly and political involvement is far greater. From an open, liberal attitude, Britain has become more defensive, and more apprehensive, so that there are fewer areas to operate in and reduced scope for Chinese engagement. In the finance sector, apart from the more niche area of RMB trading, there has been a similar retrenchment. This is less about Brexit and London no longer being as straightforward a platform as it once was to enter Europe and more about the general geopolitical environment, with deteriorating US–China relations looming large. Even in the once hallowed field of intellectual engagement and research collaboration, the situation is more vexed than it once was. British universities and educational establishments are challenged as never before to justify their links with China. This is occurring at the same time as the numbers of British learning Chinese, while modestly rising at least at school level, are still only a tiny proportion of what they need to be. While British berate themselves for their lack of knowledge and what is called "China competence capacity", at the same time those from Britain that do choose to go along this path are met with high levels of suspicion and scrutiny than ever before. Never before has the complexity of UK–China relations been so great, so confusing and so full of contradictions. And yet, never before have the British been so inadequately equipped to deal with this.

4

Walk on by: what does Britain really want from China?

In 2019, I attended a conference at Cambridge University. We were well looked after at the college we were staying at. Academics, policy-makers, company representatives made for an eclectic mix. The main theme everyone present was pondering was the shape of geopolitics after disruptive events from Brexit in the UK to Trump in the US, and rising tensions with powers labelled authoritarian and autocratic. Of these, Russia and China took pride of place.

One of the key attendees was someone who, at that time, was a government minister. They appeared halfway through the event, their entourage hovering around them as they entered the seminar room. After making brief remarks about how they saw the world, someone took them to task for the government's stance on leaving the EU. As a businessperson, they said, they saw nothing good about what was trying to be achieved in getting out of the single market and imposing barriers to trade with our greatest partners, in terms of volume at least. The politician listened politely, but was clearly not there to change their mind – nor did they give much impression they were going to change anyone else's. "We are where we are", they said in response.

It was only after this that I felt emboldened to raise my hand and ask a vaguely related follow-up question. "In view of the fact that our relationship with Europe is already complicated, and likely to get even more so, one assumes that creating closer links with emerging economies like China's makes sense. What do you think the government and Britain want from China?" The politician gazed at me a little bemused, looked down at the sheet of papers in front of them, and in a somewhat dismissive, tired voice simple stated, "Well, nothing really. We don't want anything from them!"

In the previous 12 months I had travelled across much of the world, attending events and seminars about China, in places as far afield as Kuala Lumpa, Singapore, Manila, Thessaloniki, Ankara, Oslo, New York and San Paolo. Each of these had one thing in common: China *mattered*. The question was one of degree. In Manila, speaking with the local Ministry of Foreign Affairs, it was about how to balance the Philippines' long, deep and extensive relationship with the United States with the need, despite having limited capacity, to gain more from the commercial relationship with their huge regional neighbour, only a few hundred kilometres across the South China Sea. For Singapore, at a major conference on the Belt and Road Initiative, it was a question of how best to continue being close to both Washington and Beijing – particularly in view of the increasing pressure on the city state by the country that claimed to be the ancestral origin of most of its population. In New Zealand, in the almost impossibly natural beauty of the Southern Islands, the anxiety was palpable at a meeting of business and government figures who were experiencing the attentions of the People's Republic as never before. Malaysia was still dealing with the impact of the missing Malaysian Airlines Flight 370, on which many Chinese tourists were travelling, which had simply vanished in 2014. Feelings towards China were more ambiguous there. But in none of these places did I ever hear someone declare so categorically that they wanted nothing from China. Only back home, in the UK, would I get to hear such blunt, almost hubristic sentiments.

That minister was simply wrong in their answer – or being deliberately provocative. If Asia was the frontline of hard thinking about China's emerging power because of its direct experience with things that China was doing economically, and the US was equally engaged almost to the point of panic in the face of this rising, looming, very different power now competing with them (in their eyes), then Europe and North America were a fairly febrile second front. In Vancouver – often called a Chinese paradise because of the combination of excellent Chinese food, great weather, and a large émigré population – at a business conference where the usual discourse would have been warm platitudes and friendly words, the young, newly arrived Chinese ambassador berated the audience of Canadians for sticking by outmoded, old-fashioned ideas about his country. The familiar critique of Chinese human rights and governance issues was evidently no longer so easily tolerated by its target. In

Brazil, the tone was less sharp, but the worry was still there – of an Asian country which had simply come from nowhere in the last few years to be the largest user of their exported commodities and a major economic partner. China's difference with Brazil, despite sharing BRICS status, was that they had, at least for the moment, managed to maintain high growth and not sink into a debilitating and destabilizing recession. That was a cause of considerable envy and admiration in Sao Paolo. The issue for Brazilians was a critical lack of expertise about how to best speak to and understand China. In Europe, either inside or outside the EU, things were perhaps even more layered and bewildering. Serbians in Belgrade, an accession state to the great Union project, were lobbying relentlessly for Chinese sources of investment for sectors like airports and railways. Athens had succeeded in getting Chinese money, with some success, into the port of Piraeus, and had been so aligned with Chinese interests that it had blocked an EU wide démarche on human rights issues in June 2017, to the bitter disappointment of NGOs and others. For Denmark, the conference hosted by a Confucius Institute provided an overview of local media coverage of the Chinese influence now emerging. The conclusion was clear: this was a problematic issue, with most domestic coverage critical and negative, despite Chinese attempts to be more involved in the local economy still somewhat limited. Riga, the beautiful, ancient Latvian capital, maintained a more idealistic, lofty view of the potential largesse from the Far East, possibly because of the realization that most Chinese would not even know how to find it on a map.

Every place had people who gave nuanced responses and held a slightly different position on this question. For some, China was a reality in people's daily lives through being owner of infrastructure or companies, or the major source of tourists and students. In others, the focus was more on the potential relationship rather than the actual one. The one common thread connecting all these diverse, very different locations was that in all of them, more and more people were thinking about China (and often thinking so much that their governments, universities, or businesses were funding major conferences to which were invited an international set of experts) and, at the same time, in all of them, while articulated differently, there was distrust towards China, confusion about its intentions, and a lack of consensus about its aims. In no place did anyone, at any time, say that China was not relevant and important.

China itself and its messaging was a frequent source of this confusion. Almost overnight, the country has gone from being confined largely to its own space, with no real links to the wider world (in 1966, because of turbulence back home, there was only one ambassador from China serving abroad – Huang Hua, in Egypt), to being the largest trading partners of over 120 countries. From next to no international travel for its citizens in the 1980s, it had risen to being amongst the largest suppliers of international tourists (and often the highest spending) at least in the years leading up to the Covid-19 pandemic. Had this sort of accelerated rise been experienced by a country that shared the same political system and broad outlook as the current group of developed economies that would have been disruptive enough. Witness the travails undergone by democratic and economically liberal Japan in the late 1980s when it looked poised to take over the United States as the world's largest economy. But the kind of differences in its political system already outlined about China makes accommodating its new status and importance for others even more challenging.

These problems of distrust and lack of knowledge meant it was often hard to pick apart the instances where countries were talking about their perception of their own vulnerabilities, and how any emerging major country could raise questions about these (New Zealand, for instance, and its isolation, and small population) and where they were referring to real, evidence-based issues about specific Chinese behaviour and demands. More often than not, the main worries related to concerns about how Beijing was using its economic clout to enforce agreement with its line on such issues as the South or East China Sea, Tibet, Xinjiang or Taiwan. Another strand of worries was about the use of telecommunications companies like Huawei and others to be part of a major state-led push by China in the virtual world, sucking up intellectual property and other intelligence information under the rest of the world's noses. What was much rarer, at least at this stage, were concerns that China was trying to destabilize or disorder democratic countries in ways that resembled attempts that happened in the Cold War, or even along the lines Russia is accused of to this day. On the whole, China's domestic challenges, and its desire for a predictable external world, mean that many felt that it didn't involve itself to a great extent in the kind of ideological and political battles outside its borders that sought to change people's minds about their own systems. It seemed to have a lofty disdain for the kinds of politics Europeans or Americans practice and had come to the (probably correct) conclusion, after the more adventurous Maoist years when there were brief attempts to export its indigenous ideology, that foreigners cannot and will never be converted to the wisdom of Marxism with Chinese characteristics. And yet, by 2025, even this notion was undermined by many making passionate arguments that China was out to remould and recreate the West and infiltrate its political systems, through concerted efforts by the United Front Department.[1]

The minister breezily declaring in 2019 at the Cambridge seminar that the UK did not want anything in particular from China had given a statement that was as erroneous in terms of history as it was geopolitically. Britain after all had had some recent experience at working out very specific things that it wanted and how it might be able to get them from China in a level of detail perhaps far deeper than many other powers. Over the future fate of Hong Kong, from the 1970s onwards, British officials had to think hard first about how to preserve the city's unique structure as it came to the end of over a century and a half of colonial rule from London and reverted to Chinese sovereignty, and how to negotiate with Chinese partners to achieve this. This was a very clear goal, with very particular parameters. The objective moved swiftly in 1982 when Margaret Thatcher as prime minister became fully engaged with the issue and went to Beijing to discuss it with the then Chinese paramount leader Deng Xiaoping. Initially, she had believed that China might grant continuing, extended leases for British control of the city. She was quickly disabused of that idea when Deng declared that sovereign control by China was non-negotiable. It subsequently became an issue of preserving the legal, economic and to some extent social and political status quo as far as possible. With that objective in mind, Whitehall mandarins like Percy Craddock sat down to business with their Chinese counterparts. They achieved most of their aims with the 1984 agreement, which accepted that Hong Kong, for 50 years after 1997 and retrocession, would enjoy a high degree of autonomy.

Hong Kong, however, was a very specific matter and one in which Britain had no choice but to get involved. On the far broader question of what the UK wants from the People's Republic today, things are more complex and much less clear. And in any case, the situation in Hong

Kong showed that even a good agreement can fray and start to dramatically change well into its timeframe. By 2020, the city was prey to far more Beijing intervention, with political activists and democracy party figures being jailed, or fleeing the city, or simply ceasing their activity. As Craddock and others acknowledged after the event, Britain negotiated from a weak position (China said it would simply send troops in to retake the city in 1997 whether Britain agreed a deal with it or not). We know today that it achieved at least 20 years of some sort of meaningful autonomy. That was less than was hoped for but more than perhaps many expected.

GETTING COMPLICATED

Looking back to 2019 the discussion of what Britain wanted from China then now seems very remote. At that time, one had an unwieldy constellation of different actors to factor in, with their different expectations and demands along with whether there was alignment with what China wanted from the UK. But despite this complicated set up, talk of investment, finance and technology or intellectual partnership covered most of the relevant areas. But the securitization of UK–China relations and the more turbulent geopolitics subsequently has meant that the discussion today has been wholly reframed. There is still some consensus, despite the cabinet minister's airy dismissal, earlier mentioned, of China's relevance to the UK's needs, that Britain does want something. This was why the 2021 Integrated Review, and then the refresh of this in 2023 mapped out a framework where in some areas there was alignment. But at the same time there is a far greater acknowledgement of there being instances where Britain competes with China, and plenty of other areas where it needs to protect itself against China. Thus the "protect, align, engage" mantra.

The Integrated Review's main purpose was to attempt to set out an overarching narrative for Britain's international relations. This was an implicit admission that as a middle-ranking power, the need to find strength in numbers by working with allies and similar-minded nations against those who did not share the same liberal values and outlook had become more urgent. The days of working with China, as the aim had been in the 2000s, to build civil society, its legal system, and the broad foundations of greater participation in decision making and democracy were over. Xi Jinping's government brought about the removal of any doubt on this front – China was not in the business of allowing engagement which it viewed as having ulterior, political motives. Reinforcing the notions of greater Chinese cultural confidence formulated from the 1990s by the chief ideologue sitting in the Politburo, Wang Huning, Chinese officials issued instructions demanding a rejection of Western universalism, and a pushback against all forms of external ideological influence in classrooms and lecture halls. The now infamous Document Number Nine issued in 2013 made this rebuttal clear:

> Given Western nations' long-term dominance in the realms of economics, military affairs, science, and technology, these arguments [about the dominance and universal applicability of Western notions of freedom, human rights and justice] can be confusing and deceptive. The goal [of such slogans] is to obscure the essential differences between the West's value system and the value system we advocate, ultimately using the West's value systems to supplant the core values of Socialism.[2]

According to this outlook, the espousal of these causes by the US, UK and others was nothing more than a Trojan horse to try to make the country lose its own identity and once more become prey to Western dominance and interference. On top of the pushback from within China, the West had limited resources after the 2008 financial crash to influence the PRC through economic incentives as its own resources and capacities came under pressure. This created a two-way street: just as the West increasingly made clear there were things it did and did *not* want from China, so China reciprocated. It too was in the business of being selective, making clear the parameters of engagement it believed worked for it. Both sides were now in a more defensive position.

Ideally, and in the simplest terms, within the "Engage" box are the more transactional things that Britain seeks from China. That covers investment – although in increasingly restricted sectors. It also covers simple trading in goods – although the persistent trade imbalance in China's favour remains. In 2021, according to the British Office for National Statistics, China was the largest British source of imports, and the sixth largest for exports. Britain imported £63 billion worth of goods, most of it machinery, telecoms and office equipment. It exported fuel, machinery and cars.[3] Services were only a small proportion of exports, mostly in the travel sector. From a peak in 2021, overall trade volumes between both countries fell to about 5 per cent less for both of the successive years.[4] Investment has already been discussed in the previous chapter. Despite earlier high expectations, by 2024 China was not a significant deployer of FDI in Britain. Nor did Britain have a great deal of its investment running the other way, with only 0.6 per cent (about £11.2 billion) of the global stock of its commitments in the People's Republic.[5]

Britain also has an interest in the technology that China is producing. This falls more into the "Align" area. Its greatest common interests are in addressing global issues. Of these, climate change and the environment are perhaps the most important and the highest profile. With Donald Trump's first presidency in 2017, and his withdrawal from the Paris convention on climate change agreed two years before, China became an increasingly important player in this space. From his time as Party Secretary of the prosperous and highly industrialized province of Zhejiang between 2002 and 2007, Xi Jinping had been a vocal supporter of greening the economy. In power, he maintained this commitment, no doubt bolstered by the fact that it was a core interest for the people he might claim to be his most important supporters – the urban-living, service-sector-working middle class emerging in the country. For these, a clean environment with good quality air, water and soil was imperative. In all of these areas, rapid development over the last few decades had caused widespread and at times calamitous degradation.

Xi burnished his credentials as an internationalist when addressing the Global Economic Forum at Davos in 2017. It was to be a brief moment when China's international image improved as the United States settled into a far more fractious, isolationist frame of mind under Trump. The trade wars, perceptions of China's growing nationalistic posture towards its neighbours, and its more assertive foreign policy, sitting alongside a widespread deterioration of confidence in the political West, meant that by 2020 most of that positive image for the People's Republic had disappeared. But even in the most difficult moments, China maintained its environmental dialogue with others and participated proactively in the various United Nations Climate Change Conference of the Parties (COPs) meetings. Even as the UK was producing harsher national security legislation towards China and making the decision to insist Huawei components be removed from G5 equipment, the overall tone of its collaboration with Beijing in this area remained positive. A range of programmes from those aiming to achieve Net Zero in carbon emissions to greening of cities, and energy efficient building, were rolled out from 2021. Even the Chinese media was keen to broadcast news about this area of mutual work, with the state-owned *Global Times* declaring in May 2024 that "As major economies, China and the UK have significant influence in promoting green transition. Green cooperation between the two countries has huge potential in the eyes of industrial players and policymakers".[6] Green finance was one key area, with London seeing the issuance of green and sustainable developments bonds coming from Chinese financial institutions, amounting to £12 billion by 2024.

COMMON FEARS

In a book on the key issues posing an existential threat to humanity, Oxford academic Toby Ord set rising sea levels and hotter climate alongside the risks of a pandemic, a meteor hitting the earth, and devastation from a nuclear war. Of this horrendous and sobering menu of calamities, he assessed that artificial intelligence (AI) was the most immediately threatening, and that it was only a matter of years rather than decades before humans created entities that, on some levels at least, would be able to outperform them – and function without them.[7] China is already a global player in AI research and development, producing by 2021, according to one report from the consultancy McKinsey, a third of paper journal articles on AI and the same proportion of citations. It also accounted for a fifth of global investment in AI, with $16 billion committed to start-ups in the same year.[8] In this sector, Britain is similarly a significant player, although not on the scale of China, with investment by the end of 2024 of about $4.4 billion.[9]

Like China, the UK wrestles with the implications of AI. Convening the AI Safety Summit in November 2023 at Bletchley Park in Britain, the

British government (despite reservations from Japan) invited Chinese representatives. In a joint statement issued at the end of the meeting the attendees stated that "particular safety risks arise at the 'frontier' of AI, understood as being those highly capable general-purpose AI models, including foundation models, that could perform a wide variety of tasks – as well as relevant specific narrow AI that could exhibit capabilities that cause harm – which match or exceed the capabilities present in today's most advanced models". The statement went on:

> We are especially concerned by such risks in domains such as cybersecurity and biotechnology, as well as where frontier AI systems may amplify risks such as disinformation. There is potential for serious, even catastrophic, harm, either deliberate or unintentional, stemming from the most significant capabilities of these AI models. Given the rapid and uncertain rate of change of AI, and in the context of the acceleration of investment in technology, we affirm that deepening our understanding of these potential risks and of actions to address them is especially urgent.[10]

Once more, for any hope of coordinated, global action against these dangers, China was clearly an indispensable partner.

Britain also needed, whether it liked it or not, Chinese cooperation on terrorism, and on combatting international crime. On money laundering, in 2019 when the then Chinese Vice Premier Hu Chunhua visited Britain, a memorandum of understanding about how best to cooperate was mooted, though no steps were subsequently taken to achieve this. In 2016, summits were held on combatting corruption, and on security. A China–UK High Level Security Dialogue convened in 2016 also covered joint work against terrorism. The second was held a year later. These lapsed after that date. In fact, it was more about how Britain could defend itself against claimed Chinese interference and intrusion that became the priority. The whole question of what Britain wanted from China had therefore shifted, in a few years, from a list of positive things, to the very different, albeit related question of what it *did not* want. This too was a kind of desire, only a negative one. Therein came the whole "protect" agenda.

From 2018, largely through increased influence from the US and its security concerns about China, spelt out most starkly in a speech made by the then US Vice President Mike Spence, the UK posture largely changed from the positive one outlined in the "Golden Era" to something highly defensive and securitized. Pence had stated at the Hudson Institute, the US think tank, that "as we speak, Beijing is employing a whole-of-government approach, using political, economic, and military tools, as well as propaganda, to advance its influence and benefit its interests in the United States".[11] From that point, many British politicians started to adopt a similarly suspicious attitude towards China. There are too many examples to try to cite here. The government of Theresa May had largely been trying to work on the idea of a post-Brexit trade deal with the PRC. While not formally signing anything on collaboration on the Belt and Road Initiative, in a visit to China in early 2018 her spokespeople stated that a "joint trade and investment review which will now take place as the first step towards delivering ambitious future trade arrangements".[12] But within the space of 18 months, the posture of the UK changed. As prime minister, Boris Johnson declared himself a Sinophile. But that did little to outweigh his opportunism in trying to keep as close as possible to the US, nor help in dealing with a sizeable caucus of members of his own Conservative Party who were focused on framing China in far more hawkish, problematic terms. The establishment of the China Research Group (CRG) in 2020 signalled the first time that a coalition of parliamentarians had formally convened to focus specifically on the threats and issues that they saw China as posing. While there had long been an All Party Parliamentary Group on China, with cross-party support, this was regarded as too benign and too submissive. Instead, the CRG on their website set out three clear aims it wished to understand better and focus on:

China's industrial policy. How China's trade policy, state aid and strategic inward investments are shaping the world, not just the UK.

Technology futures. How the development, ownership and regulation of platform technologies that underpin future economic growth and innovation are being influenced.

Chinese foreign policy. The effects of "Belt and Road", China's main objectives, and where these align or clash with ours. How to understand Chinese soft power as well as hard power.[13]

Some of their members increasingly advocated a unilateral decoupling from China. Speaking on 15 April 2024, when then a security minister, one of the co-chairs of the CRG Tom Tugendhat declared that "the hostile activity we have seen from Chinese authorities and state-affiliated groups poses a serious threat to the security and wellbeing of the British people and to our partners and allies across the world".[14] His colleague, the then chair of the Foreign Affairs Select Committee, Alicia Kearns, stated that she had received threats and attacks from China-originated sources, and that the UK needed to take action to forestall these. "The threat is real, they are trying to undermine our democracy", she stated in an interview with Sky News in March 2024.[15] Iain Duncan Smith, a fellow Conservative MP, produced perhaps the most entrenched and hawkish view on China's threat to Britain. From issues like genetic data to spying in Britain, he was a ready voice for media interviews and op-eds, presenting himself as an authority on Chinese issues in Britain, and declaring in one interview in May 2024 that China was a huge threat to Britain and that its "purpose was to 'destroy democracy' and the country needs to 'take it on'".[16]

The Integrated Review sought to find a happy medium between the different competing demands for working with China. Nor should the more hawkish voices be taken as over-representative of British views. There were plenty who continued to advocate engagement and strategic alignment where possible. But by 2024, the UK had come to mirror Chinese obsessions with security, becoming far more defensive, and largely abandoning the formerly liberal position it had on commitment to open markets, a free investment environment, and research and collaboration links with China being the default rather than special cases.

China did many things to support the side of the hawks. While the jury is still out on the origins of the Covid-19 pandemic, the original handling of it by Beijing gave evidence of plenty of incompetence and lack of transparency. On top of this, the establishment of "re-education camps" in the Xinjiang area of the country from 2018 provided a constant drip-feed of examples, many of them well evidenced, of wide-spread human rights abuses. Whether the activities of the Chinese government and its officials really did constitute genocide is, as even some of the most critical of the Chinese government admitted, an issue best left to lawyers. But the sanctioning of Chinese officials associated with this issue resulted in retaliatory measures being imposed on British (and European and US) public officials. Tom Tugendhat was one of them. That meant that there were plenty of vocal figures who were all too keen to vent their anger and frustration at China, and give very precise reasons why they were doing so. The Chinese ambassador to Britain was subsequently banned from the estate of parliament, meaning that one of the world's most important economies and diplomatic players was barred from easy direct contact with the key legislative and democratic body in Britain.

Hong Kong remained a key issue. If there is one unique aspect of Sino–British relations it is the continuing importance of the city, despite retrocession occurring a quarter of a century previously. But the chaotic conditions there from 2014 onwards, with protests over political reform, and then over the imposition of new security rules, meant that by 2019 the central government adopted a far harder line. Speaking when visiting in 2022, Xi declared that the city could not afford the chaos it had experienced three years before.[17]John Lee was appointed the new Chief Executive that year, someone with a security background. It signalled that the Basic Law, which served as the de facto constitution of the city from 1997, was being interpreted in a very different way – with the onus on the preservation of stability and the needs of Beijing, rather than any special allowance made for Hong Kong itself.

Plenty of criticisms could be made for various opposition groups in Hong Kong. They had often been disunited, fractious, and in some cases unrealistic in what they might achieve and how to go about that. But the detention and then sentencing of elected officials and then those in civil society seen as critical of Beijing produced sharp international condemnation. Britain had plenty of people with a strong emotional and moral attachment to the city, and who lobbied passionately, and often effectively, for its interests. The arrival in Britain from 2021 of people from Hong Kong who were able to apply for British citizenship after five years meant that many of the most harshly treated, and therefore harshly critical of the Chinese behaviour in their home city, now advocated its cause in the UK. But it was clear that of the various things Britain did want from China, a number of public figures were convinced that defending the cause of Hong Kong and stopping the deterioration of governance in the city was one of the most important. They wanted to safeguard the moral and legal obligations for the 50-year period from 1997 after the handover. And they wanted China to abide by what they regarded as its treaty obligations. As then Foreign Secretary Dominic Raab said in 2020: "China has once again broken its promises and undermined Hong Kong's high degree of autonomy. The UK will stand up for the people of Hong Kong, and call out violations of their rights and freedoms. With our international partners, we will hold China to the obligations it freely assumed under international law."[18] In effect, what Britain was saying it wanted China to do was keep its word.

WHAT DID BRITAIN WANT FROM CHINA?

Returning to my encounter with a government minister in 2019, one can now see that their reply to the question "What does Britain want from China" of "Nothing in particular" was wrong. In fact, as so much of public discourse over this period and in the years afterwards, there was a constant tension between an increasingly complex reality and a misleading and highly simplistic rhetoric that came to dominate and distort perceptions. Britain's behaviour even during the dark days of relations with China between 2021 and 2024 showed that in areas from environment to AI it accepted the need to engage with the PRC. That was the whole point of the Integrated Review – an attempt to map out a framework that accepted the new complexity and made it manageable.

Up to 2020, one might frame Brexit as offering either a future where Britain was looking to upgrade its relations with the world's second largest economy due to expediency and the need for alternative opportunities outside the EU, or where it failed to grasp these and found the negative economic impact of exiting the single market even greater. I confess that at this time I was sceptical that Britain would be able to achieve a good quality trade deal with China, but to be fair, I was also sceptical that Britain would seek to leave the EU with the kind of harder edged deal it subsequently arranged. What I did not foresee (and I was in good company here – most others failed to see this too) was the array of other factors that weighed in on the China issue. Of these, the posture of the US was perhaps the easiest to discern; signs of this were already in place in 2018. So too were the ways in which the Xi leadership was making it far harder for the world to relate to China more easily as it took a more assertive and confident approach to its role and its diplomacy. The game changer however was something no one could have easily forecast – the pandemic from early 2020 and its impact across the world, both on countries, and on the way they related to China. It created a paradigm shift, which was dramatic, tending to accentuate the negatives, and putting pressure on the positives. Hong Kong, Xinjiang, claims of unfair trade practices, competition across the Global South, and claims of espionage and influence in Britain itself – all these were part of the China situation for Britain before 2020, but became starker afterwards. And while the UK and China did continue to collaborate and work together, on facing the pandemic, and then on other global issues after this date, it tended to be more *sotto voce*, as though it were something people had to be defensive about rather than proud and supportive.

What did Britain want from China by 2025? After all of this, it is worth remembering that being in a tough or difficult place with the PRC is not an unusual situation for Britain. In 1967, Britain's legation offices in Beijing were burnt down by revolutionary activists. In 1999, the NATO accidental bombing of the Chinese embassy in Belgrade, Serbia resulted in stones being thrown at the British embassy in Beijing, and protestors assembling at its gates. In 2012, there were months when Britain and China had no high-level contact because of Cameron's meeting with the Dalai Lama. All of this indicated a relationship that was fundamentally fractious and unstable, and had been structured not on any positive vision of the two sides being aligned or the same, but on an acceptance of precisely the opposite – that they were profoundly unaligned and different, but in many areas had no choice but to work with each other.

Standing back from all of this, one can discern the real tramlines of Sino–UK relations. What Britain had always wanted from China, even when it was at the peak of its powers there in the nineteenth century, was a place that was amenable to its interests, that was not so strong that it could cause problems, nor so weak as to be unstable and create issues. Britain wanted a China that worked for Britain. The issue by 2025 was that it was faced with a China that was something it had never had to deal with before – a place that was stronger than it, and able to dictate rather than be dictated to. That perhaps explains the wounded, almost irritated tone of some of the most viscerally critical of China and its role and links with Britain. For them, the default was very much a world where Britain was the giver of lectures and instructions, and China the receiver – willingly or reluctantly. By 2025, for the UK at least (and probably for everyone else) that world had gone. In its posture on China, Britain was often disorientated and contradictory, which will be addressed in the final chapter.

Who cares? China and the British people

For much of my career dealing with China in various guises and ways since my first visit to the country in 1991, I have sought to get British people, and particularly those identified as influential, to take more notice of China and give it greater priority in our national lives. In 2018, for a Chinese publisher, I wrote an autobiographical account of how my own engagement with the culture and life of this extraordinary place had developed.[1] In that book, while writing it, I reflected on how it was perfectly possible to go through the education system in the UK in the 1970s into the 1990s and have next to no idea, at the end of it, of anything much about the history and politics even of modern China, let alone its long past. Granted, that was probably true of a lot of other places too. India, Russia, the Middle East, all received patchy coverage. But in terms of my own path, I had ended up attending an elite university (Cambridge) and graduating with only a vague awareness that there was this place on the other side of the world, that had a turbulent history in the last century, that was currently governed by a communist party, and that was very different to Britain. The most I could say is that I had some general idea that there had been a few points of connection, and that there were places like Chinatown in London, or galleries in the British Museum, where one might experience and have direct contact with what could be very loosely described as Chinese culture and heritage. But beyond this generality it was hard to say anything concrete or empirical.

Of course, this dearth of information about a remote and very different place was down to much more than just indifference on the side of the British. Language learning across the board (including European tongues) was declining, particularly from the 2000s. History departments at universities were being closed down for lack of students.

Education was undergoing almost perpetual and radical change. Even so, the intuition that China as (at the time) the most populous country in the world, and one that was clearly becoming increasingly influential, but no less different for all of that in terms of values and priorities, merited more attention never left me. From the 1990s into the 2000s, as a diplomat, and then working at a think tank, and finally as an academic, one of my functions, I believed, was to raise awareness in Britain, at schools, universities, amongst any circles I could get access to, that Britain had to do more to be knowledgeable about this country, and that it was in our national interest to shed some of our provinciality and give a bit more space and attention to what was happening there. China, as one British official more far sighted than I in the early 2000s stated to me during a discussion, was the first country in modern history to have risen to such a level of global prominence with a fundamentally different view of the world. This was not just political. In terms of values and beliefs, the Chinese-speaking world with its own canonical texts for philosophy from the Confucian and legalist traditions, its hybrid views on religion (the three great teachings of Confucius, Buddhism and Daoism existing side by side with no real attempt to opt for one above the others in the last millennium and a half) presented plenty of evidence it was certainly different from that of Enlightenment Europe. The question was how to frame and understand this difference, and to avoid simply "othering" the place and seeing it as some total alternative to what existed in the political West.

Paradoxically, while knowledge levels of Chinese language (as discussed in Chatper 3) have fallen, China itself has attracted more attention since 2018, becoming framed in terms outlined in the previous chapters as Britain's greatest security challenge (by some) and a problem in swathes of other areas from technology to geopolitics. It seems the more we need to know about the place as it rises in importance, the less we want to know. Our ignorance appears as willed and deliberate, rather than accidental and unconscious. There was a prefiguring of the current situation. Briefly, in 2008, at the time of the Beijing Olympics, I encountered a number of people at events and in the media starting to opine on China. The torch relay ceremony drew widespread demonstrations across the United States and Europe, serving as a particular lightning rod because of China's human rights issues. But once the Olympics were over, the global attention shifted elsewhere (to the Arab Springs in the Middle East, to the perpetual economic crisis in Europe, and then, further down the line, to the Russian encroachments on Crimea). China sank into the background again. But in 2020, with the pandemic, attention returned and was more sustained. China was a major news story, with politicians willing to devote time and space in the UK to speaking about an issue they rarely engaged with. It led to a fresh awareness of how much, in terms of manufacturing and supply chains, China had influence. A generation of commentators and activists, many of whom had never visited nor studied the place, and who could not speak a word of Chinese, suddenly became zealous advocates of "waking up" to this looming threat. The world I once hoped for, of people speaking about China, being interested in the country, and finding it influential and important, had arrived. The problem was that their attitudes were almost always overwhelmingly negative and antagonistic. It was not to engage with China and work out a reciprocal framework that they wanted. Such pragmatism for them was a dirty word. What was necessary was to start defending Britain against this "invasion" of an alien power with self-serving ambitions and aims.

The net result of this whole process is that, in 2025, the "China circle" in Britain – those groups of people engaged in the economic, political, cultural and knowledge links with the People's Republic – has indeed broadened. It has undergone the same process of complexification as was noted in the previous two chapters on the questions of what both places want from each other.

In the third decade of the twenty-first century, of those who currently actually deal with China, who are the main "stakeholders" in the relationship, there is a mixture of longstanding groups. They are listed below. But they are joined by some new arrivals, and the issue is increasingly how hard it is to create a workable consensus amongst these. As in other areas of national life, divisions have grown broader, more visible, and in some cases deeper. There is a spectrum of those with a largely benign, sympathetic attitude towards China, who believe it has been victimized and demonized by the West, and then there are those who sit somewhere in the middle of this, and try to achieve a level of neutrality, and finally those who are adamant that China is almost at the level of an existential threat, that it harbours malign intent, and that we are in a situation akin to a second Cold War, only this time far more complex.

One thing I did not appreciate when writing of the UK-related China groups even a few years ago was that this spectrum had good antecedents, and ones that typified Europe generally, rather than just Britain. From the first records of sustained encounters with China around the time of the Jesuit missionaries and then traders that went there in the sixteenth century, the information they brought or sent back to Europe about the so called "celestial empire" with its self-contained, ancient and sophisticated culture and politics (in their eyes) was interpreted in broadly three different ways. These can best be described through the views of three great Enlightenment figures who symbolize the contrasting postures. On the one hand, the French thinker Voltaire, at least in the early part of his life, held China up as the example of a meritocratic system, one that offered much for Europeans to emulate, particularly in its largely secular nature. His aim was the despotic influence of the Catholic Church, which was the target of much of his criticism. In many ways, China figured in much of his writing in a highly idealised form. For an opposite view, one can look at his close contemporary, and compatriot, the political philosopher Montesquieu, who portrayed China as a place typifying despotism and absolute rule of emperors against the individual rights of citizens. They could both be categorized as sceptics, people who regarded China with deep reservations and suspicion, and felt it was a premodern place, and one that needed to undergo fundamental reform. Between these two stood the German philosopher Leibniz, who strove, in a series of writings inspired from the testimony of Jesuits based in China and sent back to Europe in the early eighteenth century, to gain an objective, more empirical understanding of what China was and what its people believed. He in many ways represented the realists.

Idealists, sceptics and realists – this broad grouping remains with us today. Despite the vast changes in so many areas in the intervening centuries, European views of China, and British views as a subset of these, remain divided. On the whole, the sceptics have usually had the most influence. The idealists and empiricists have both tended to be in the minority. The puzzle, however, is why these divisions remain in view of the massive increase in direct contact and access. The simple truth is that today, with so much more information, from so many more sources, with more Chinese in the UK than ever before, and with many more means of traveling to China and seeing the place directly, to remain unaware or indifferent to the place is a deliberate act of will. Once one had to work to be knowledgeable about the People's Republic. Now one has to put real effort into being ignorant of it. But despite this, many still achieve the latter. We shall discuss this group later, because their lack of knowledge has not prevented them from issuing opinions and views about the country, and seeking to have influence over British attitudes towards it.

The first group of people (or networks) in Britan that is readily identifiable as those who have professional reasons to know about China, in some cases to study the Chinese language, visit the country and regularly interact with Chinese partners are people like me: professional sinologists working in universities, commentators on Chinese affairs, authors of books on China, teachers of Chinese in colleges and schools. This is not a large group of people, and alas it seems to be shrinking. According to one report, the number of universities offering single honours undergraduate degrees in Chinese studies fell from 13 to nine in the space of 12 months from September 2019 to September 2020.[2] An annual survey of Chinese studies in Britain by the British Association of Chinese Studies in 2021 pointed out that, as with many other subject areas, numbers of teaching staff had fallen in universities, with a 31 per cent drop in staff numbers despite a rise in student ratios.[3] Moreover, the teaching body is, as of 2025, a largely international cohort. The blunt fact is that Britain produces precious few sinologists, a point made previously. As one American colleague at a UK university said, pointing to me at a conference in 2018, "You are looking at a two horned unicorn – a British-born sinologist!" Of the directors of the four main university centres in the UK dealing with China, to the best of my knowledge, at the time of writing, I am the sole Brit. One was born in Hong Kong, the other is from the US, and the third is European. Many colleagues occupying university positions dealing with China are originally from the Chinese-speaking world. Another colleague as long as 20 years ago acknowledged this, saying laconically that the sheer effort and difficulty of learning written and spoken Chinese was enough of an impediment to mean that expertise in the UK was largely imported. And after all, with so many Chinese students studying at British universities from the early

2000s, it was inevitable that some of those would want to continue their academic careers in the UK. That is precisely what happened. And it is a good job they chose to do so, as Britain would never have produced enough people with the requisite language skills to fill these university positions. From the position where, in the early nineteenth century, people like Robert Morrison, the compiler of the first Chinese–English dictionary, Thomas Wade, Herbert Giles and others pioneered sinology in Britain at the same time as there was almost no similar capacity in China, the situation is reversed. In 2025 when, rightly or wrongly, China is labelled a security threat, an economic rival, a matter of international and national importance in terms of technology, geopolitical strategy and sustainability, Britain produces not more, but fewer sinologists from its universities than it did at the turn of the century when the Chinese economy was still smaller than the UK's. To add to these woes, the funding for Chinese studies is reducing, with even those that do raise financial support for Chairs and endowed positions subject to innuendo-led and highly politicized attacks, which results in support being even more circumscribed and threatened. This is nothing short of a pedagogical and intellectual scandal.

Beyond this largely universities-based group are officials in government departments. As in the past, when Britain ran the largest consular network in the world across Qing China in the late nineteenth century, it was the government system that tended to produce people with lived experience of China and linguistic skills in Chinese. Embassies and consulates in China and Hong Kong were growing, as links between the two countries increased over the decades up to 2015. These were staffed by specialists and generalists from different government departments, or from organizations on secondment. Within the Diplomatic Service there were those who, by accident or design, have made knowledge about China a core competency – the China cadre. In other government departments, today, it is increasingly common to come across those who either studied Chinese for a degree, or who have lived there, or who have some other demonstrable link. In departments of trade, foreign affairs, domestic affairs, culture and media – almost all areas now – having knowledge of the People's Republic is helpful, and for these people dealing with China, either through hosting delegations or even being involved in negotiating bilateral arrangements, the value of this knowledge is increasing. For this group, China figures as a player they need to understand and factor into their daily lives, and while some of their work and careers are spent outside the UK, they feed intimately into the UK's policy responses to China, and spend considerable parts of their lives back at home. This group too, however, is under threat. The UK Foreign Office reportedly now trains, annually, only 14 staff to communicate in Mandarin Chinese as of 2022.[4] The pandemic and the freezing of contact with Chinese officialdom under Xi Jinping meant that from 2020, representation in the country inevitably reduced. On a visit to Beijing in August 2024, the first for five years because of the restrictions on travel due to the pandemic, I was struck by the lack of contact between British officials serving there and their Chinese counterparts. Other conversations showed that the general securitization of all issues to do with China from the UK (and of course the Chinese) side, meant that those with any extensive experience in China over the previous few decades (people, for instance, like me) were regarded as a potential security problem, and found it hard to get clearance even if they did want to enter government service in the People's Republic for the UK. Remarkably, one of the key people who had worked in this capacity over previous years told me they had been informed that they would not, under current arrangements, be able to work in any government capacity for Britain dealing with China. So to add to the crisis of producing sinologists in Britain is added the fact that one of the very few alternative routes to Chinese expertise – government service – is now also not offering a sustainable career. It seems that the British government is looking for people with high levels of skills in Chinese, and real insights and understanding of the country, but who have never lived there, never had contact with Chinese people, and are running on abstractions and theories. Such people, alas, do not exist.

The same general shrinking of space goes for a cohort of businesspeople. Some have investments in China, some run joint ventures, others have offices there, or are looking for business there. For this group, China was or could be a source of trade, goods and services, profit, even capital (more and more are seeking investment from China). These people were supported by trade associations, chambers of commerce in major Chinese cities, and groups supporting specific sectors like aviation, automotive and financial services. The heyday years from China's entry to the

WTO in 2001 to the "Golden Era" in 2015 were ones where businesses hoped to find a foothold in China, with an eye on the great emerging middle class there as potential customers and clients. Consultants and advisors, many based in the UK, attempted to help them. This was never a huge group of people. With the Trump trade wars, and the pandemic, it too has shrunk. Entities like the China–Britian Business Council, a partially British government-funded entity, continue to promote business opportunities, but once more, beyond the key players who, through thick and thin, were always in China like HSBC, Standard Chartered, Rolls Royce and BP, this cohort too is smaller than it was ten years ago. Even on these meagre returns, they remain constantly vulnerable to shrill denunciations by the most hawkish voices in the UK who inevitably use the stale line that, as ever, Britain is putting profit above principle in dealing with China. The underlying truth of the current situation is that there is precious little profit, and that in any case, as pointed out in Chapter 1, in 400 years of engagement with China, Britain even when it had massive strength was little interested in promoting values. It wanted to make money. The anomaly in the twenty-first century is that at a time when the UK has seldom been economically weaker, and its imbalances with China in this area never before wider, it has chosen the period of maximum vulnerability to start preaching and moralizing. That seems a strange strategy to adopt. It has so far produced zero results, beyond a warm feeling of self-righteousness. Business groups mirror the general shrinkage of the Chinese circle seen in professional and government circles.

It would be good to know if the other area of Chinese information and expertise – the media – at least enjoyed some expansion in the post-"Golden Era". Journalists after all were similar to officials in often having lived experience in the PRC, some of it extensive and wide ranging. But once more, it is contraction, not expansion, that one sees here. Journalists were present in Beijing working for British outlets, or from Britain, for all of the period after 1950. In the Cultural Revolution, Anthony Grey, while working for Reuters, was imprisoned for two years in Beijing between 1967 and 1969. Figures like David Bonavia of *The Times* were key disseminators of information about China in the years when it was undergoing reform and opening up. But by 2025, partly through the influence of the pandemic, and partly through the rising tensions between the PRC and the political West, the number of accredited journalists working in China had fallen, rather than risen. A great deal of this can be blamed on the Chinese government, whose frustrations with the ways in which these journalists failed to treat it, in their eyes, fairly, led to campaigns of harassment and intimidation against precisely the people who could give publicity to this. John Studworth of the BBC had to flee to Taiwan in 2021 after concluding that the country was too dangerous for him and his family to continue working there. And while the *Financial Times* and *The Economist* (at least till 2024) did maintain representation in the country, many outlets like *The Guardian* and *The Times* had to cover the country either from Hong Kong, or from Taiwan.

That has meant a great deal of reportage and analysis of China has ended up emanating from people not inside the country, and often going from second- or third-hand sources. Again, one needs to stress that the Chinese government was as much the author of this situation as anyone else. But it meant that in the British media (and others for that matter) the general tone and content of stories about China was usually negative. On the whole, journalism became as politicized as other areas, with many getting their information about China from social media with widely varying editorial standards and accuracy. Those working in what is dismissively called the "legacy media" were existing in a more and more threatened space by 2024 and its tradition of high-quality journalism about China was simply a part of this larger story, with very few outlets able to commit the capacity to unearth good stories about the place, and a general lack of sources within the country to offer anything credible on which to base these.

There is, however, one area in the China circle in Britain that has expanded in the decade after 2015 – lobby groups. Some of these have existed for a long time. Those related to Tibet, for instance, and to the broader issue of human rights in China. There are groups with long-standing expertise on, for example, the environment, or legal reform. From 2015, however, a host of other groups came into existence, some with a specific focus on issues like Hong Kong, or on university study and funding related to China. Within parliament, the China Research Group (CRG), already mentioned, was formed, with some emulation of the European Research Group which had been credited with leading to the rise of antipathy to the European Union, the 2016 membership referendum, and ultimately to the decision to leave. Issues like the repression of people of mostly Uyghur ethnicity in Xinjiang attracted attention from Amnesty International and Human Rights Watch. Although both desisted from deploying the term genocide to describe the actions of the Chinese government there, lobby groups were successful in getting the British parliament to pass a motion on Xinjiang that did label it as genocide in April 2021, just as they also could claim some success in bringing about a higher profile for the issue of Hong Kong and its citizens.

Lobby groups might be worthy and their work important. They are part of any democracy. But they are also promoting specific views, and inevitably at times these are partial, or partisan. They exist after all to do this kind of work. The greater and more urgent they can make the issue they focus on, the more support and profile it will get. Governments have to engage in dialogue with such groups, not allow them unilaterally to run policy. Engagement with China, as this book has argued, is a complex issue. It involves balancing an increasingly difficult and at times clashing set of interests and risks. The intense securitization of many aspects of Britain's relations with China, the problematic nature of the Xi regime and its more nationalist and populist, confident tone, and the general contraction of other areas of Chinese expertise in the UK offering different perspectives, has meant that by 2025, lobby groups with often narrow and sometimes highly selective agendas were able to exert disproportionate influence over public opinion and, at times, government policy and its implementation. Through social media they were able to mount campaigns in which, at times, almost anyone linked with China, unless they did not engage in fierce public criticism of the current regime, was regarded as an appeaser. I write from personal experience of this, and know just how unsettling it can be.

The final key group in the China circle in the UK are people of Chinese heritage. The first person from China recorded as coming to the UK was in the 1680s when Shen Fuzhong, a Christian convert, worked in Oxford for a year or so. After that time and until the end of the nineteenth century, there were very limited numbers of people in the UK of Chinese heritage. One of the reasons for this was simply that the Qing authorities forbade their citizens from leaving the empire and then returning. It was only in 1850 that a Chinese person first studied at a British university

(Edinburgh) and only in the 1870s that a Chinese representative office was set up in London, leading to a full embassy soon afterwards. Chinatowns were established primarily because of sea trade and the arrival of sailors who sometimes settled in Britain, first at Liverpool, and then in London. The site of the latter, which had 300 people of Chinese heritage in 1910, was originally in the Limehouse area of the East End, a place now memorialized by street names like Peking Road and Amoy Street. British trade unions in particular did not view the arrival of such people kindly – in 1909 there were riots by striking seamen in Cardiff who destroyed many of the laundries run by Chinese settlers there. Until the 1948 British Nationality Act, a British women who married a foreign man, including a Chinese man, would lose her British citizenship. By the 1940s, the numbers of Chinese in the UK had dwindled to the extent that they were almost non-existent. It was only during the 1950s that the British Chinese population began to rise, following a sustained economic downturn in Hong Kong causing a new group of immigrants to come to Britain. Many of this first generation famously opened takeaways, and through this became part of national life. But their children tended to end up working in professions from medicine to law to accountancy and academia. What was striking was that even by 2000, when around 300,000 people in Britain identified as of Chinese heritage, they did not participate in political life. Until the 2000s, there had never been a person of Chinese ethnicity who was elected to parliament. With the Conservative MP Alan Mak that changed in 2015. Only in July 2024 was the first person born in China elected to parliament – Yuan Yang, Labour MP for Earley and Woodley. Whether people of British Chinese heritage will enjoy the same kind of profile as those of Indian heritage, or African for that matter, remains to be seen.

What has changed in a relatively short space of time is the influx of over 150,000 people from Hong Kong as a result of the new rules passed in 2021. These people are, of course, culturally and ethnically Chinese. But the reason most have come to Britain is because of deep (and well-founded) dissatisfaction with the situation in their home city and the increased controls exercised by the Chinese central government. Many like Nathan Law, a former student leader of groups supporting democratic reform in Hong Kong, are activists in the UK now, passionately advocating the cause of their city and the need for the UK to support its democratic development. Laudable as these aims are, they too are only partially representative of the UK's broader interests in China. Hong Kong, after all, is a part of the overall British relationship rather than its whole focus, and in many ways perhaps one of diminishing importance. The days in which Hong Kong was regarded as a portal to China were coming to an end even before 1997. Increasingly since that time, for business, and for any other activity, direct access and contact with the rest of the country was possible, and preferable. Many Hong Kongese are listened to and have a platform in Britian when they speak about UK–China relations because they are regarded as knowledgeable and authoritative. Most British people after all would have limited knowledge about how Hong Kong is different from China, and the historic background of the city, beyond some idea that it was once a colony of Britain. But Hong Kong was always and remains to some extent a very different place to the rest of China, and assuming that people from the city are straightforwardly representative of China generally and that they understand the Chinese political system is as erroneous as believing that passionate advocates of Scottish independence based in the US are a good guide to what is happening in Westminster national politics in Britain.

This simple audit shows that from the beginning of the so-called "Golden Era" to 2025 (the space of a mere ten years) despite the complexity of issues involving China for Britain getting even greater, and despite the widespread acknowledgement that there was a critical need for good quality analysis and evidence-based understanding, in almost all areas this had reduced and diminished. There were fewer people in Chinese studies coming from British universities, fewer jobs for those wanting to go into academia once they came through this, fewer business positions, fewer officials who had a Chinese background who might be able to go to China and work, and fewer journalists from Britain based in China. Lobby groups had increased, and so too, largely through the Hong Kong scheme, had the number of people of Chinese heritage. But, for the reasons outlined above, as a potential source of advice and counsel these were not unproblematic.

A ROD FOR OUR BACKS: THE POLITICIZATION OF CHINA

In the past, particularly after the Second World War, the victory of the Communists in China meant that one of the main areas of support for the new regime and China circles in Britain was based on political sympathy. Figures as august as the great Cambridge sinologist Joseph Needham were, by their own admission, highly committed to a vision of equality, of moderate socialism, and of China being accorded a just outcome after its tragic encounter with colonialization and oppression. The Cambridge economist Joan Robinson also saw in the creation of the People's Republic the manifestation of dreams for a better society, where China would lead the way. During the Cultural Revolution, when most were simply not allowed into the country, Robinson and others participated in study tours. Figures like fellow Cantabrigian and Nobel Prize-winner Philip Noel-Baker took part in events like these in which they sometimes breathlessly reported on the progress being made in Mao's China, enthusiastically describing communities and other highly managed sites they were able to visit.[5] Groups like the Society for Anglo-Chinese Understanding and the British Council for International Trade with China, a trading organization established in London in the 1950s, were set up partly to express solidarity with the Chinese people, and their struggle for emancipation. The infamous so-called "Red Dean of Canterbury", Hewlett Johnson, was even accorded a personal meeting with Mao Zedong during a visit there in 1962.[6] This is recognition that the issue of China in Britain even before today, has often been a highly politicized one. It was frequently one that involved people having to take a position on whether they were supportive, or antagonistic, to what the new Chinese authorities were trying to do.

After Mao's death, these groups were lambasted as more news came to light of the atrocities that had been committed in China during his reign. But the craze for Maoism was never anywhere near as intense in the UK as it was, for instance, in France, where figures like the philosophers Simone de Beauvoir, Jean-Paul Sartre and Julia Kristeva all, at some stage or another, expressed Maoist sympathies.[7] Direct engagement with China, unless one were a government official and had to do it as part of one's job, was highly politicized, and engagement with the country's contemporary situation usually signalled, rightly or wrongly, something about one's political inclinations being a motivation for doing this. Chinese authorities did not, during the later years of Mao's life, particularly help this situation, with their support in London of Red Guard-like demonstrations emanating from the Portland Place Legation (the most famous scuffle of this was in August 1967), and insistence that only those willing to proffer sincere friendship and support for the Beijing regime could get into their country.

With a more outward looking and open China from the late 1970s, at least in terms of the movement of people and access, this should have changed. After all, Deng's pragmatism undermined almost everything that Mao had stood for, from embracing marketization to allowing for a non-state sector to emerge. China's strategy of engagement meant it was seeking a new community to speak to – scientists, technicians, policy-makers – those who held some practical, rather than ideological interest for it, as it tried to build its material capacity. Even so, the maintenance, despite everything, of a one-party monopoly on power in China remained a great sticking point for Western democracies and still does. That means that while those specializing in Europe, North America or other similar multi-party democratic environments do not get asked to defend the systems they are talking about but asked just to analyse and describe it, China specialists, willingly or unwillingly, often get dragged into debates about the rights or wrongs of the Chinese political system per se and its record on human rights. Frequently specialists are accused of being sympathizers and promoters of the communist regime in this effort to explain it. This issue has always been present. The main change by 2025 is that it has grown considerably sharper and more obvious.

This is not to deny that China's political system *is* an issue. The one thing many people will know about the country is that it still operates under a communist government. And that plays into a whole history of negative impressions and ideas about Marxism as a form of administration associated with, for instance, the Soviet Union, the Cold War, and the collapse of the Iron Curtain, that many British have (and Europeans or Americans for that matter). That China still maintains this system is something that was evidently not meant to happen (see the discussion of engagement and its guiding philosophy covered earlier). This explains why trying to speak neutrally or without value judgements about China is sometimes attacked as defending the place and its leaders. But given how important a balanced understanding and analysis which is seen as trustworthy and neutral about the People's Republic now is, it is a problem that China remains such a politicized issue. In other academic areas we accept individuals may have private political convictions, but that these should play no role in their professional work. Some years ago when criticized for his widely known sympathy for right-wing politics and that this prevented him from writing history impartially, Niall Ferguson pointed out that when going to a doctor, their political opinions were of no import – it was their diagnostic and medical skills that mattered. He argued that the same applied for an historian. They could hold whatever personal beliefs they wanted; the main thing was to be logical, evidence based, and meticulous in their argumentation. For a sinologist too, or for anyone speaking about China as an expert, it should also be like this. Whether supportive or not of the project of bringing communism with Chinese characteristics to life, the main thing is to maintain a divide between one's personal belief, or non-belief, in this and one's attempts to portray Chinese politics and contemporary issues accurately and with good explanatory frameworks. Even so, there can be few other geographies which entail this risk of being labelled a supporter or critic, with the labels "pro-" or "anti-" China bandied about nonchalantly.

IMPROVING THE WORLD'S CHINA DISCOURSE

Whether we like it or not (and it seems a large number of people don't), China is part of the lives of people across the world. It is not somewhere people need to make an effort to go and seek, but a place that is coming to them, through what they buy (much of it imported from the PRC), through where they send their children to university (where there are almost inevitably going to be Chinese students in attendance), through the environment they live in and the way that China's environmental issues impact on that. If they use TikTok, or DeepSeek, or BYD electric cars, or order online from Shein, then, willing or not, China is reaching into their lives. And yet, the claim of this book is that the communities that are most engaged with China in the UK are small, often marginalized, politicized, and more often than not so highly specialized as to be inaccessible. What is more, they are becoming smaller and more beleaguered and threatened. This is an intimidating list of disadvantages. Anyone from outside this coterie with no previous experience would therefore have good reason to regard getting more interested in China and trying to learn more about the country, despite its new prominence in their lives, frustrating and dishearteningly difficult. They are very likely to be informed that the language is fiendishly hard, that the country has alien political values, and that it would take a life-time of monk-like devotion to truly understand it properly. In light of this, the surprise is not that so few people, in places like the UK, make an attempt to master Mandarin and come to know the country better, but that so many do, despite this list of horrendous impediments. The success of the British Council's programme, Generation UK, to facilitate British students going to China for language learning, exposure and experience which has run from 2013 and taken 55,000 young people on internships and study programmes testifies to this.[8] So too is the Mandarin Excellence programme which teaches the language to 15,000 school children in Britain. There is a cohort of British who really do want to do something about learning, engaging with, and understanding China, and do so with open minds and real adventurousness and commitment. The question is whether the far larger majority of their compatriots can start to emulate them, and what sort of structures and support needs to be put in place to make this happen.

That this needs to happen is self-evident. As things stand in 2025, the UK is attempting to deal with a complex, rapidly developing issue, but with methods and human capital resources that are more fitting for the previous century, and more appropriate for understanding a country that is tiny, marginal and less important than it now is, and not the most populous in the world, a far larger geopolitical player and a much bigger economy. And it is doing so with a discourse that is frequently over-specialized, or politicized, with accretions from history that desperately need clearing away. The use of a more accessible, clearer, and more mainstream discourse on China – and here discourse means not just things said, but the knowledge, the way in which ideas are conveyed and the frameworks they are presented in, and the emotions they involve – is urgent.

In Chinese philosophy, at the time of the ancient Confucians, there was "the doctrine of the names" that maintained that without use of the right words, how could ideas ever be correct or accurate. Confucius himself in the *Analects* stated that "they who do not understand words, cannot understand people".[9] Words are more often than not the entry into someone's soul, their inner life. But they have to be interpreted in the right way, and the language used itself has to be flexible, subtle and precise. Because language about China is often jumbled up, and laden with value judgements, or segregated into highly specialist discourses, is it any wonder that the British have great challenges in trying to work out the best set of questions that they need to address. The previous chapters outlined some ideas about what China broadly wants from the UK, and what the UK might want from China, and how these have become increasingly complex, and at times contradictory. The UK has no hope of implementing a workable policy approach towards China where risks and opportunities can be segregated and managed, and balanced with its many other international interests and commitments, without a pool of people who don't just have China "capacity" (the current favoured lingo in government circles) but some degree of China wisdom. That means perspective, nuance, and an ability to have some empathy with Chinese even if this runs alongside clear acceptance of differences and disagreements. The strategic choice has become very clear under Xi Jinping, particularly for a middle-ranking power like Britain with limited leverage on its own. It can certainly berate China and condemn it for its many issues in Hong Kong, Xinjiang, towards Taiwan, and within its own domestic politics. But whether that will bring about any meaningful outcome in terms of changes in China's behaviour for the better is a moot point. One wonders whether, since 2000, there has been a single case of British official condemnation of China, on its own, bringing about any change in the minds or actions of the Chinese government. That itself must give us pause for thought.

The majority recognize, however, that, as the previous chapters have outlined, Britain faces a range of issues that requires a relationship with China and some level of collaboration and dialogue, whether it likes it or not. That means it needs people who can undertake this work. As of 2025, the situation is growing close to calamitous. Never before has China posed so many challenges and tricky questions for the UK. And never before has Britian had less qualified people to deal with this. Instead, paradoxically, many of the commentators found daily in social media and in print speaking about China have opinions and no direct experience, attitudes and no knowledge, and posture rather than promote real solutions. While they berate the government for having no coherent policy towards China, they show almost no understanding of how a good policy is not just something that exists on paper, but has to be carried into practice. That means it needs people to go and make it real, knowing what they are doing, and being able to negotiate with the Chinese. It is perverse indeed that a combination of security and other worries means that some of the very few people who might be able to do this, can't. To paraphrase the cricket analogy of the former Foreign Secretary Geoffrey Howe when resigning from Margarat Thatcher's government in 1990, it is as though the team captain is sending key players on to the field, having previously broken their bats. That is precisely the situation that Britain is in today as it seeks to engage and manage its relations with China.

Britain's China future in the world of Brexit, Trump and Xi Jinping

The striking characteristic of British relations with China in the decade since 2015 is how what was once a persistently fractious, difficult, complex relationship travelled from a period of idealism, optimism and hyper-engagement, to almost the complete opposite. That itself is an aberration. Few countries in their links with China can have experienced such a rollercoaster. Throughout this period, the UK was in a similar position to many others in the West in trying to understand a new world where a power like China with such different outlook, political values and aspirations to its own was becoming increasingly important. In 2020, the UK was doing this while undertaking its own readjustment and re-evaluation of its place in the world because of the impact of Brexit. But quickly, to this situation was added the Sino–US trade wars and the collateral that came from them, then the pandemic and its impact, and then the Russian invasion of Ukraine in 2022 and how that influenced geopolitics. In view of all of these, it is not surprising that the "Golden Era" rhetoric and expectations soon became outmoded.

As much by necessity as for any other reason, what all of this did achieve was to force British politicians to think about China in a more complex and more urgent way. That had good and bad aspects. James Cleverly, when serving as British Foreign Secretary in 2023, delivered a statement on Britain's position on China, which offers a good starting point for a broader discussion of what the options were for its relations with China in the new context it found itself by then. Cleverly's speech was unusual in showing at least some empathy with the country and people he was talking about:

> [China's] inventions – paper, printing, gunpowder, the com-
> pass – these things transformed the fortunes of the whole
> of humanity. These innovations are the key to understanding
> why China's economy was among the biggest in the world
> for 20 of the last 22 centuries, and why China, in 1820, com-
> prised a third of global GDP – more than America, the UK
> and Europe combined.
>
> Then calamities struck, one after another; some caused by
> foreign aggression; others coming from within China itself.
> The deadliest of which was Mao's famine, which claimed tens
> of millions of lives, more than any other famine in human
> history.[1]

Cleverly followed this with an aside that was possibly aimed at critics in his own party: "If you are looking for British foreign policy by soundbite, I'm afraid you will be disappointed". This was a snappy way of saying something simpler: that the situation was complicated, and it was no use to try to ignore that.

By the time that Cleverly spoke, the aspiration that Britain, now outside the EU, might be able to forge a bilateral trade deal on its own with the PRC had largely evaporated. The European Union in late 2019 had announced the negotiation of a Common Agreement on Investment after seven years of argument and debate with their partners in Beijing. It was the first step, and a substantive one, towards opening up the critically important services sector, which now constituted over half of the Chinese economy and was seen as a future driver of growth. But the agreement was never ratified because of the sanction placed on members of the European Parliament in retaliation at similar measures being imposed on Chinese officials working in or on Xinjiang. Britain ended up therefore in a similar position. For political, rather than economic reasons, it could not even start to move towards working on a trade and services concord. Even if it had been able to, there were formidable barriers to overcome, not the least of them the fact that China as the far larger economy held most of the key negotiating cards, meaning that the likelihood of Britain achieving a balanced, reasonable deal was low before actual negotiations had even started.

THE GREAT DIVERGENCE

Many other things had changed by 2023. The mainstay of UK–China ties from the handover of Hong Kong in 1997 to at least the early 2010s had largely been about both sides working for mutual economic benefit – largely ignoring the issues around values and security where there were clearly major differences of understanding. For the UK over this period this all occurred at the same time as it was a member of the European Union. Practically that meant that in talking about economic links, and trying to place pressure on China, the UK did so as part of the world's largest and wealthiest single market, the EU-27. This gave it enhanced leverage than if it simply tried to achieve things bilaterally. The benefits of this were proved by the successful battles with China over textiles (the so-called "bra wars" in the 2000s) and then the fight over solar power panels in 2012, which was once more resolved after fierce verbal clashes between both sides. In each case, manufacturers in China were accused of flooding the European market with goods that were exported at prices considerably cheaper than they had been to make because of subsidies and benefits given out by the Chinese state. In both cases, the EU collectively bargained with partners in the Chinese government and by threatening the use of tariffs and other punitive responses managed, in the end, to settle. In the first dispute, the Chinese agreed to cease exporting certain classes of goods like pullovers and jumpers from 2006 because of complaints about their non-market prices by competitors in Europe. In the second, from 2013, new more realistic prices were agreed with Chinese suppliers for solar panels that competed with EU-made ones. The EU market, and the EU's collective intellectual property powers, mattered to China, as disputes like these and the compromises finally reached proved. So while it might have been happy to single out one member state for harsh treatment, it would very likely think twice about punishing the whole of the bloc. The EU accounted, after all, for over €450 billion of China's trade per year by 2015, and a large amount of mutual investment.

The alignment between the UK and EU on China worked at a conceptual level. For all the bilateral competition, with ministers from member states traipsing to Beijing almost daily to promote their national interests, when one looks at a document like the 2006 statement issued by the European Commission, "The EU and China: Closer Partners, Growing Responsibilities", the core interests prefigure those that the UK articulated three years later in the Foreign Office document, "The UK and China: A Framework for Engagement".[2] These were: (1) supporting China's transition towards a more open and plural society; (2) sustainable development; (3) trade and economic relations; (4) strengthening bilateral cooperation; and (5) international and regional cooperation.[3] The main difference is an inversion, with values placed before promotion of economic interests, unlike the British iteration which turned these the other way around. It had set out three key areas: getting the best for UK's growth; fostering China's emergence as a responsible global player; and promoting sustainable development. By 2016, when the next statement of a similar status was issued by the EU, this list of interests had become more granular. In the "Communication on China", ironically published the very same day as the outcome of the UK referendum became known, the "Principles of Engagement" section set out the following holistic framework:

> The fundamental principle of the EU's relationship with China is that it should be based on reciprocal benefit in both political and economic terms.
>
> – The EU's engagement with China should be principled, practical and pragmatic, staying true to its interests and values. It will continue to be based on a positive agenda of partnership coupled with the constructive management of differences.
> – EU Member States' engagement with China must comply with EU laws, rules and policies.
> – The EU expects China to assume responsibilities in line with the benefits it draws from the rules-based international order.
> – The promotion of human rights will continue to be a core part of the EU's engagement with China, with the well-being of citizens and respect for international obligations at the centre of its approach. The EU will hold China to account for its human rights record.

- The EU confirms its "One China" policy.[4]
- The EU should continue to develop its relations with Taiwan and to support the constructive development of cross-Strait relations.
- The EU should support the continued implementation of "One Country, Two Systems" in Hong Kong and Macao.
- EU policy-making on China should take full account of the EU's close relationships with the US and other partners.[5]

Once more, the UK could see its ideal relationship fitting into this framework comfortably, even with the talk of a "Golden Era" promoted the year before. Just replacing "EU" in the list above with "UK" proves that. In each case, the UK could not dissent. In many ways, too, the EU offered a perfect foil for the knottier aspects of engagement – discussion of human rights, values, labour standards, and social or political values. In the era of Xi, and its more muscular attitude to the outside world, the value of this collective use of the EU as a shield to avoid the flame of targeted Chinese ire was not inconsiderable. As the number of rights lawyers being detained, journalists harassed, and dissident's and other human rights cases mounted in the PRC, it was through the EU that the most powerful denunciations were issued – and it was the EU that usually took the brunt of Chinese dissatisfaction. In 2015 alone, according to Amnesty International, 248 rights lawyers (those dealing with the most sensitive and difficult individual rights based cases) were detained by the authorities in a major summer crackdown.[6] As a creation able to irritate and frustrate the Chinese, one has to admit that Brussels, with its labyrinth of decision making, its complexity and maverick qualities was almost perfect – certainly effective enough for the Chinese government to put huge effort into trying to divide and blunt its approach. This was the suspected motive behind the Chinese desire to create a gathering of Central and Eastern European nations, "Sixteen Plus One" from 2013 onwards. This group consisted of 11 EU member states and five non-EU ones, all clustered between Germany and Russia, with a secretariat in Beijing, and at its annual high-level meeting, usually attended by the Chinese premier, the countries promoted their investment and political interests with Beijing. It is worth noting that this grouping largely fragmented and eroded after 2020.

In a strange way, the alignment with Europe does continue even after Britain exited the EU in early 2020. This is because the EU also used a trilateral division, expressing this in a document in 2019:

> Based on clearly defined interests and principles, the EU should deepen its engagement with China to promote common interests at global level. The EU should robustly seek more balanced and reciprocal conditions governing the economic relationship. Finally, in order to maintain its prosperity, values and social model over the long term, there are areas where the EU itself needs to adapt to changing economic realities and strengthen its own domestic policies and industrial base.[7]

This can be summarized as cooperate, compete and contest – not dissimilar to the protect, align and engage framework of the UK position outlined in Chapter 3. It was also echoed by the use of a similar trinity referred to by US Secretary of State Anthony Blinken in 2022 when he used the slightly different but related terms of "invest, align, compete".[8] What is striking about these different positions from the EU, Britain and America is that underneath a superficial similarity, they are clearly very broad categories that are subject to interpretation. And how these are interpreted matters hugely. One partner's competition might be another's challenge. Alignment for the US in its specific interests with China means a different thing than alignment for the EU, and for Britain. For all the appearance of conceptual commonality, underneath the rhetoric lay a far more complex reality and plenty of space for disagreement and tension. The simple fact for the UK was that as it left the EU, it was inevitably placed in a far more complex situation with China where many of the safeguards and leverage it once had had disappeared.

Britain to some extent tried to compensate for this by engaging in non-EU related forms of multilateralism. Of these, perhaps the most initially significant was AUKUS, a pact between Australia, America and itself established in 2021. The core idea of this grouping was to provide greater coherency and linkages between the three parties. The main potentially impactful aspect was the undertaking to provide Australia with nuclear powered submarines, bolstering its capacity to be a regional security player. Even on this point, however, there was scepticism about how soon this might happen, with some claiming that delivery might not be for decades. A related impact was symbolic – an attempt to give some reality to the idea that Britain was now a global player in its own right. The idea of the Indo-Pacific as a meaningful regional concept, something energetically promoted by the British government, was also a significant new development. Despite only having a small garrison in Brunei, the UK with its second aircraft carrier, HMS *Queen Elizabeth*, now started to engage in tours of duty in the region. In 2021, it did a seven-month visit, going through the Indian Ocean and the South China Sea to Japan, where it stopped off. This was to support the freedom of navigation spearheaded by the US to push back against Chinese encroachments and claims in the maritime region around its borders.

PRAGMATISM, RECIPROCITY, SUSTAINABILITY?

One of the paradoxes of British foreign policy towards China from 2015 was how, from one extreme to the other, it became, at least politically, prone to different forms of idealism – from the sunny optimism of the "Golden Era", to the demands, from 2021 to 2024, for strong assertion of values even if they carried commercial and economic costs. Historians looking back at this period may well regard it as an aberrant one, and not the norm. The disposition of British foreign policy since the time of Palmerston in the Victorian era had been a realist one. This is best illustrated by the comment in 1848, by the then Foreign Secretary, who said, "We have no eternal allies, and we have no perpetual enemies. Our interests are eternal and perpetual, and those interests it is our duty to follow". The phrase has been quoted many times ever since, despite the fact that it leaves the huge issue of what those common interests might be unanswered.

Such realism and hard-eyed pragmatism might strike some as morally problematic – but in terms of dealing with what looks like an increasingly complex future, I would argue strongly that it is the only rational approach. The situation in 2025 is an easy one to summarize. The second presidency of Donald J. Trump is likely to be turbulent and disruptive, with a continuation of US isolationism, demands that Europeans, British and others take more responsibility for their security, and sharper competition in trade and economics with China. The rest of the world will need to navigate and fit into these new parameters as best they can. They will need to balance their interests with the US and those that they have for themselves. For China, the Xi Jinping leadership so far seems to have no end in sight. There is a Congress for the Communist Party to be held in 2027. But there is little sign that anyone likely to be a successor to Xi will emerge any time soon or that there might be some form of anointment of his by then. His muscular form of nationalism with Chinese characteristics, of "Making China Great Again", is therefore likely to be a feature of geopolitics for several years ahead.

When one looks, however, at the underlying ethos of Britain's approach to China from 2015 to 2025, despite much of the surface froth, pragmatism and realism continued. It figured in James Cleverly's 2023 speech mentioned above, but also surfaced in many other statements by public figures and commentators. The recognition that the UK had to find a way to work with China, and that it was in its interests to do so, was the consensus, not the outlier. For these reasons, the UK officially engaged with China in the United Nations' COP process, and on AI. It also continued a range of other collaborations, through universities and other partners. It restarted the Economic and Financial Dialogue when Rachel Reeves visited Beijing in January 2025, the first visit by a Chancellor of the Exchequer for several years.

In 2019, I suggested that there should be three focal areas, both to structure potential scenarios and to offer a means of evaluation of the British approach towards China. These were around pragmatism, reciprocity and sustainability. I argued that the UK needed to have an approach to China that led to tangible outcomes that went beyond rhetoric, and which achieved some level of balance. For reasons that go far wider that Brexit and its impact, however, the intervening six years have delivered some harsh lessons. The reality in 2025 is that the UK has less influence economically, diplomatically, and more limited access to and leverage over China than ever before. The challenge today is not how to achieve balance – but how to shore up a far more precarious position when the UK is buffeted by headwinds from almost every direction. It is about how to at least preserve some space rather than how to try to create, and expand, others. Any effective future policy will need to be highly specific and granular to have a chance of having any impact. The era of the grand gesture towards China and of seeking to work harmoniously and embrace engagement as the default rather than the exception is now over. With the US making increasingly assertive demands about how its allies operate with what it perceives as a major challenge to its power, such broad, expansive cooperation is no longer permissible. Almost everything that is done with the PRC now needs justification and defending arguments. If there is one thing that was learned from the "Golden Era", it is that a broad-based relationship where the assumption is that cooperation is the default unless there are solid arguments otherwise is no longer possible. In almost every area, securitization, risk assessment, and cautiousness now dominate. From assuming everything is possible until told otherwise, the UK now operates from the opposite direction – everything is impossible, unless it can be proven why it needs to happen.

To some extent, many of the underlying issues with China are made trickier because they relate not just to the mechanics of how things need to happen, but relate to the question of feelings and narratives. China's difference, culturally and politically, means that it is not a partner that can be regarded with a straightforward neutrality. In many ways, Britain's more sanguine and distant view of China up to the pandemic typified this neutrality. But that situation too has radically changed. Of the various networks that constitute the China field in the UK mentioned in Chapter 5, the general public was not one of them. And yet, because of the pandemic, China began to figure far more for British people in ways that it had already for Australians and Americans, who had recognized some time before of the immediate impact of things from and about China on their own environment. Based in Australia from 2012 to 2015 I was struck by the fact that local people at that time had an emotional response to China, even if sometimes an antagonistic and negative one. The place mattered enough to them for them to feel something towards it. In the UK, when I came back in 2015, that element felt missing. British people largely harboured indifferent attitudes towards China. They did not respond to news about it with the sort of heightened sense of anxiety of interest as Australians often did. They seemed, on the whole, almost languid.

This was one reason why the "Golden Era" was strange. Its use of often highly-charged terms and phrases which seemed to indicate enthusiasm and some kind of warmth were not met with any real public acceptance of this. It was as though the British government were trying to arouse feelings that needed response and involvement from an audience that largely regarded themselves as disinterested bystanders. There was a high level of detachment. With the pandemic that changed. China's problems and issues became problems and issues for British people. Surveys that had shown reasonable levels of favourability about Chinese investment but more negative attitudes elsewhere became far more streamlined. A YouGov survey in 2022 found that 75 per cent held a negative attitude with a quarter of respondents regarding China as an "enemy".[9] In May 2020 at the height of the pandemic's first wave, another survey showed 83 per cent of those spoken to did not trust China.[10] The stark reality was that the more British knew about China, the less they seemed to like what they were hearing, something compounded by the fact that they felt their lives were impacted by events in the PRC, leading to them suffering lockdowns and economic hardship. Even the attempts by China to send personal protection equipment to Europe and the UK did little to alleviate this sense of anger and resentment.

One way of avoiding the relationship becoming simply a matter of emotions and emotional responses and instead giving it greater depth and sustainability is to understand better what the British story of China was. As Chapter 1 showed, the two countries were hardly new to each other. They hadn't magically discovered one another in the twenty-first century and were working things out from scratch. They had links going back hundreds of years. They had left in imprint on each other. A British narrative about China was something that even government officials were working on. One of those who spoke to me about this some time later said that while it was difficult to capture this story easily, what was clear in all the polling and analysis available to them was, whatever the age group or demographic sector surveyed, British people regarded China as remote and unknowable. That implied that it was distrusted as much because British people felt they could not relate to it, or understand it, or felt they had no real link with it that meant anything to them, as for any reason relating directly to what China was in itself. A more concerted attempt in the education system to make China more familiar by focusing on its shared history with the UK and the influence both countries have had on each other might be one place to start in building a British story about China that helps orientate people and frame their understanding of the relationship today.

The "Golden Era" grand narrative about China, or the attempts to construct one, showed the limits of a more ambitious, wholesale approach where aspirations were high, as the notion that this related to people more generally was left behind. It did not prove sustainable simply because many people did not find it believable, or for that matter, relevant. That meant that once it was buffeted by events it had to be eventually jettisoned. It had no real viable foundations. Despite this, the period after 2015 when this grand experiment was tried did provide a precious opportunity for the UK to understand and know itself a bit better regarding its aims and attitudes towards China. It showed that under the placid surface, responses to China when they came were qualified, and apprehensive. For many, there was an ugly side to this, with claims that the sort of Sinophobia that had plagued much discourse in the early twentieth century was making an unwelcome reappearance. The "yellow peril" discourse associated with nativists and racists in the 1920s and 1930s, some of it expressed in the infamous portrayal of the fictional figure of Fu Manchu in the novels of Henry Ward, under the penname Sax Rohmer, is a well-known example of this. By the twenty-first century, events like the pandemic did prompt some claims against China that verged on the abusive and discriminatory. And while harder to prove, some of the fiercest attacks on China and its role in Britain, in universities, in business, or even in public life, seemed to display an element of anxiety and opposition to the rise of a non-European, non-North American country as a potential global leader rather than anything else.

These are complex issues where the evidence is often ambiguous and hard to interpret clearly. What is easier to argue is that the British had to face the complexity of their own position in the world with a new sense of realism. Their policy response therefore needed to be pragmatic, not in the sense of focusing on specific investment and trade outcomes that worked for its own self interest with China (although that was important) but with a sense of flexibility and responsiveness to an ever-changing terrain. Britain had to face a rapidly shifting environment in which there was a constant need for calibration and alertness to the need to create new objectives, new themes and new modes of acting. It was almost as though it now needed to engage in guerilla diplomacy.

America, China, Europe, and the whole global environment were changing in ways that were bewildering and unsettling. The grand narrative of
benign globalization had ended. Now there was something more akin to
a free for all where the sole guiding aim was to be clear to yourself about
what you needed to get out of the general situation, and, for that matter,
how you needed to avoid being sucked into destructive fights with others. Environmental and AI-related issues had wider buy in (although not
inevitably so) than trade and security issues. It was as though on every
issue, a bespoke approach had to be created. Post-pandemic, post-Brexit
Britain was one that existed in a golden age, not for UK–China relations,
but for the constant management and attentiveness of diplomacy.

INTO THE FUTURE

Trump's second presidency alone poses a host of questions for Britain.
The president is known to be highly transactional. He is forever search-
ing for an angle or a deal. If Britain occupies any space in his worldview
beyond his well-documented love of golf in Scotland and his admiration for the late Queen, it is as a place that is expected to be loyal. This
is unlikely to get in the way as he searches for the great aim – a huge
new deal with the world's second largest economy which can be spun as
in America's favour. No one knows what might be in such a deal. That
might become clear as and when Trump meets Xi Jinping. But being able
to burnish himself as the person who finally gets even with Beijing, and
even better, got one up on them would be the great prize. The United
States is a far more important market and investment destination for
China, after all. As already stated, in addition to the $600 billion (about
£475 billion) of two-way trade each year (which puts the £89 billion from
Q3 2022 to Q3 2023 for Sino–British trade in the shade), China made
$28 billion (£23 billion) of direct investment into America in 2023 (the
UK received £4.2 billion from China in the same year).[11] However, as is
the case with the UK, proportionally Chinese investment in the US is a
small fraction of the overall amount of over $5 trillion that it has from
other countries.

Britain as a medium-sized player will need to achieve some dex-
trous diplomacy in trying to achieve a balance between US and China.

This is particularly the case now that both countries are, in different ways, demanding allegiance and imposing restrictions on what countries can or can't do with others if they are to stay in their good books. Overwhelmingly, for cultural, linguistic and security reasons, Britain's default position is to stick close to the US. That makes complete sense. But dealing with a far more unilateralist, protectionist and self-interested America no longer much interested in being the world's police force and supplying public goods is something new. In the past, Britian did manage to maintain at least some space for promoting its own bilateral interests with China (these were mostly trade and investment focused, as, for instance, its joining the Asia Infrastructure Investment Bank in 2015 despite American annoyance) but the space for that is likely to shrink even further. It might even disappear.

President Macron of France had talked ambitiously of Europe having strategic autonomy in 2017. The concept was widely discussed, but also criticized. Many did not take seriously the idea that Europe could have the political and diplomatic unity to achieve a distinctive approach of its own which might directly contradict or run against that of the US. For a start it had no meaningful hard power when compared to America, and through NATO was dependent on American military might. Trump's threat to exit NATO in 2018 (a threat he has repeated since) was avoided by member states increasing their defence spending. If the EU with its far larger economy and capacity was not able to face down Trump, what hope for Britain? The brutal reality is that if it has strategic sovereignty, a great deal of that seems to be at the US's behest. Intelligence sharing for instance through the Five Eyes arrangement means Britain (and Australia, Canada and New Zealand) get access to America's formidable resources in this area. Losing this would be a massive blow. The dilemma is that with China, the options for flexibility, which were never that great, have largely shrunk even more at the same time as the American line has hardened so that it is now much like that of China, and almost completely focused on its own self-interest. In this context, the range of options for the UK in its bilateral relationship are limited. Its hands in many areas are tied. Ironically, leaving the EU has not been a liberation even in this area. Inside or outside the EU, its plight is the same.

What does the future hold for Britain and China? In some ways, the UK has arrived at a moment of harsh truth – but more about itself than the partnerships it is engaged with. The UK's anaemic growth over the past decade has presented the new Labour government in 2024 with an urgent and simple aim to kickstart economic growth. Previous attempts to improve productivity by removing red tape, and increasing business incentives were hamstrung by a domestic politics whose divisions were clearly shown by the voting outcomes of the 2024 elections. Labour won a landslide on a historically low proportion of the electorate – a little above a third of all those who cast a vote. Reform, a new, insurgent populist party, managed to get over 3 million votes, and yet only a handful of seats, raising questions about the equity of the system itself when so many seemed disenfranchised. The perpetual crisis of the National Health Service was distilled in the 7 million-strong waiting list for procedures, and wait times in hospital Accident and Emergency departments at the end of 2024 that could be counted in days, not hours. Planning restrictions have meant the second high-speed rail link north shrunk each year in terms of extent, as its costs exploded, and its finishing date extended further into the future. A planned third runway at Heathrow airport, under discussion since the early 2000s, looked no nearer to happening despite declarations in early 2025 that it was back on the cards. British universities saw their finances tumble, their global rankings fall, and their cohort of international students dwindle. Small companies complained about how their biggest overseas markets in the EU were now blocked to them by red tape and tariffs post-Brexit. And non-European inward immigration figures which had risen to record numbers in the early 2020s were a source of constant political argument and populist anger.

In this beleaguered context, the questions that China seemed to raise for Britain were all too often conflated and mixed up with how it felt about itself. For some reason, China's difference raised uneasiness and anxiety about Britain's own sense of identity and its place in the world. China figured as the spectre of a very different vision of politics, world order and identity, something that represented all too well the emergence of a new geopolitical and economic reality that was strange, alienating and unsettling for Britain's more traditional worldview. Plenty of other countries were in the same boat here. But for Britain with its history, its recent experiences, its unique set of relationships with America, the EU and China, things were more complex and therefore even more troubling. All too often, China tiggered a deeper anxiety that went beyond the nature of its relationship with the UK. It was not so much what this country the other side of the world was, and how it impacted on Britain, but more about how it made Britain feel and the confusion that its new prominence gave rise to. Britain had once been confident about its handling of this relationship. By 2025, that confidence had largely gone.

What is abundantly clear in 2025 is that the kinds of "chop and choose" options that were possible even a few years before, where Britain could declare that it could work with China where it wanted, but reject it where it felt no alignment, now sound like language from another age. With the US slapping tariffs on goods with both Europe and the UK, as never before the UK is caught in the cross hairs. Put bluntly, it has limited options and they are narrowing by the day. Like the US, its one guiding principle has to be to forever keep sight of what in the end is its national interest. And there, it has alignment with China, and the US – the wellbeing and prosperity of its own people. That means being clear sighted about the need to find sources of growth, to do so recognizing that China is now a major technology and innovation partner, and that Britain needs to find a framework no longer mired in the tired, nostalgic ethos of trying to fight battles on the moral high ground, one that was never an easy balancing act for it. In the "Golden Era", Britain's intentions were right, even if its execution failed. It was an attempt to make a new, bolder and more pragmatic relationship with a partner that it had known a long time, and was now connected with in a radically transformed way because power had shifted so decisively from it to the other. Instead of bickering over a new Chinese embassy in London, and fixating on moralizing about China's human rights failures and spying forays, Britain needs to remember one central lesson China can teach it today: that without a viable, strong, growing economy, Britain will forever be on the back foot. It needs political leadership that will tell Britain to believe in who they are and the power of their own values, and not to fear that these will be eroded by confidently, proactively engaging with China. Britain has massive assets intellectually, and a rich, complex and long history with China. It can do far, far better than its current, tepid, half-hearted, forever ambiguous position. But that needs recognition right from the start that a relationship with China for Britain is not an option but a necessity. And one that for 450 years Britain has managed. Britain doesn't need to be defeatist. It just has to recognize that we must, and can, engage with this crucial relationship, and do well from it.

Further reading

The Great Reversal: Britain, China and the 400-Year Contest for Power (London: Yale University Press, 2024), which I wrote in 2023 after a year-long sabbatical, is the first comprehensive history of the bilateral relationship to have appeared since 1911. That sets out what might be called the British China story, from the 1600s to the present. There are a number of excellent studies about specific aspects of the colonial experience of Britain in China, and with China, in the work of Robert Bickers: *Empire Made Me: An Englishman Adrift in Shanghai* (2003), *The Scramble for China: Foreign Devils in the Qing Empire, 1832–1914* (2011) and *Getting Stuck in for Shanghai: Putting the Kibosh on the Kaiser from the Bund* (2014), all published by Allen Lane.

Donna Brunero, *Britain's Imperial Cornerstone in China: The Chinese Maritime Customs Service, 1854–1949* (London: Routledge, 2006) deals with one of the main planks of the British engagement in pre-People's Republic China – the customs service and the archives in English that this left behind. Doyenne of sinology between Britain and China for the last 60 years or more is the great Wang Gungwu, whose *Anglo-Chinese Encounters since 1800: War, Trade, Science, and Governance* (Cambridge: Cambridge University Press, 2003) is one of the most authoritative accounts. For the Opium Wars and Britain's role, Julie Lovell, *The Opium Wars* (London: Picador, 2011) is beautifully written.

Robert Boardman, *Britain and the People's Republic of China, 1949–1974* (London: Macmillan, 1976) and Shaun Breslin, "Beyond diplomacy? UK relations with China since 1997", *British Journal of Politics & International Relations* 6:3 (2004): 409–25 are useful, though much has happened since they were written. My own *What's Wrong With Diplomacy? The Future of Diplomacy and the Case of China and the UK*

(London: Penguin, 2015) is a polemical account of pre-Brexit relations between the UK and China. To this can be added *Erase and Rewind: The UK and China Search for a New Framework* (Sydney: ACRI, 2016).

Notes

PREFACE

1. "Trump makes clear EU won't escape his ire over trade for long". Bloomberg, 31 August 2018: https://www.bloomberg.com/politics/articles/ 2018-08-31/trump-makes-clear-eu-won-t-escape-his-ire-over-trade-for-long?embedded-checkout=true.
2. George Osborne, "Let's create a golden decade for the UK–China relationship". Gov.UK, 22 September 2015. https://www.gov.uk/government/speeches/ chancellor-lets-create-a-golden-decade-for-the-uk-china-relationship.
3. "Covid-19 pandemic: China 'refused to give data' to WHO team". BBC, 14 February 2021. https://www.bbc.co.uk/news/world-asia-china-56054468.
4. "Trump angers Beijing with 'Chinese virus' tweet". BBC, 17 March 2020. https://www.bbc.co.uk/news/world-asia-india-51928011.
5. Rishi Sunak: "Golden era of UK–China relations is over". BBC, 29 November 2022. https://www.bbc.co.uk/news/uk-politics-63787877.
6. House of Commons Library, "Visas, security and access to services for Hongkongers living in the UK". https://commonslibrary.parliament.uk/ research-briefings/cdp-2024-0129/#:~:text=Over%20150%2C000%20 people%20have%20since,British%20citizenship%20after%20six%20years.
7. Cabinet Office, *Integrated Review Refresh 2023: Responding to a More Contested and Volatile World*. March 2023. https://assets.publishing. service.gov.uk/media/641d72f45155a2000c6ad5d5/11857435_NS_IR_ Refresh_2023_Supply_AllPages_Revision_7_WEB_PDF.pdf.
8. Fintan Smith, "A quarter of Britons consider China to be an enemy of the UK". YouGov, 14 October 2022. https://yougov.co.uk/politics/article s/44064-quarter-britons-consider-china-be-enemy-uk.

CHAPTER 1

1. A discussion of this sense of historic inevitability and the feelings it gives rise to in contemporary China and its cultural and political impact is found in my own *China's Dream: The Culture of the Communist Party and its Secret Sources of Power* (Cambridge: Polity, 2018).
2. "Government Response to the Intelligence and Security Committee of Parliament Report 'China'". September 2023. https://assets.publishing.service.gov.uk/media/6502c367702634001389b818/HM_Government_Response_to_the_ISC_Report__China_.pdf.

CHAPTER 2

1. See Todd Hall, *Emotional Diplomacy* (Ithaca, NY: Cornell University Press, 2015) for a scholarly account of the deployment of this kind of high-level emotional blackmail.
2. William Callahan has written extensively about this issue, most fully in *China: The Pessoptimist Nation* (Oxford: Oxford University Press, 2008).
3. The stark exception to this pattern was Douglas Hurd, Foreign Secretary from 1989 to 1995, who had served as a diplomat in Beijing in the 1950s.
4. For an overview of where Hong Kong currently stands, see Tim Summers, *China's Hong Kong*, second edition (Newcastle upon Tyne: Agenda, 2021).
5. See, for instance, Peter Foster, "George Osborne praised by China for ignoring human rights", *Daily Telegraph*, 25 September 2015; Isabel Hilton, Jonathan Fenby & Robert Barnett, "Has Britain sold out to Beijing?", *Foreign Policy*, 23 October 2015.
6. Rosa Freedman, "Britain sells out on human rights for Chinese investment". The Conversation, 19 October 2015. https://theconversation.com/britain-sells-out-on-human-rights-for-chinese-investment-49379.
7. "Address by the President of the People's Republic of China". Parliament of Australia, 17 November 2014. https://www.aph.gov.au/Parliamentary_Business/Hansard/Hansard_Display?bid=chamber/hansardr/35c9c2cf-9347-4a82-be89-20df5f76529b/&sid=0001.
8. The *Daily Mail*, one of the most widely read newspapers in the UK, with an online version that is globally successful, offers many excellent examples of this. From 2018 alone: "Chinese company builds a 350ft artificial waterfall" (23 July); "World's largest mosquito caught in China" (23 April); "Giant swing opens on the edge of a 1000ft high cliff in China" (4 May); "Chinese

pupils queue up to be whipped by their teacher" (16 July). While there are plenty of similar stories for the United States and Europe, for these there are at least counterbalancing pieces on trade and the economy. With China, unless it related to the trade war with the US, these were far sparser.

9. China Research Group, "Briefing: Confucius Institutes in the UK". No date. https://taiwaninsight.org/wp-content/uploads/2023/03/1239c-confucius institutes-chinaresearchgroup-june2022.pdf.

10. "Confucius Institutes". https://stratcomcoe.org/cuploads/pfiles/confucius_ institutes.pdf.

11. See "China says Sino-British Joint Declaration on Hong Kong no longer has meaning". Reuters, 30 June 2017. https://www.reuters.com/article/ world/china-says-sino-british-joint-declaration-on-hong-kong-no-longer-has-meaning-idUSKBN19L1J1/.

12. Edward Wong, "Queen Elizabeth II says Chinese officials were 'very rude' on state visit". *New York Times*, 11 May 2016. https://www.nytimes. com/2016/05/12/world/asia/china-britain-queen-xi-jinping.html.

13. To be fair, Chinese visits anywhere at this level are heavily controlled events, with nothing left to chance. This is even more the case since the occasion of the one incontrovertible example of real public feeling towards a Chinese leader while in the UK – the hurling of a shoe by an angry member of the audience during a talk given by Wen Jiabao in Cambridge in 2008.

14. UK Trade and Investment, "Chinese state visit: up to £40 billion deals agreed". Gov.UK, 23 October 2015. https://www.gov.uk/government/ news/chinese-state-visit-up-to-40-billion-deals-agreed

15. *Ibid.*

16. "Chinese CGN halts funding for UK's Hinckley Point nuclear plant". Bloomberg, 14 December 2023. https://www.bloomberg.com/news/articles/ 2023-12-13/hinkley-point-nuclear-plant-in-uk-stops-getting-funding-from-china-s-cgn.

17. See Liu Xiaoming, "Hinkley Point is a test of mutual trust between the UK and China". *Financial Times*, 8 August 2016.

18. Nick Timothy, "The Government is selling our national security to China". Conservative Home, 20 October 2015. https://www.conservativehome. com/thecolumnists/2015/10/nick-timothy-the-government-is-selling-our-national-security-to-china.html.

19. Conservative Party Human Rights Commission, "The darkest moment: the crackdown on human rights in China 2013–2016". http://www. conservativehumanrights.com/reports/submissions/CPHRC_China_ Human_Rights_Report_Final.pdf.

20. European Commission, "Joint Communication to the European Parliament and the Council: Elements for a New EU Strategy on China". 22 June 2016. http://eeas.europa.eu/archives/docs/china/docs/joint_communication_to_the_european_parliament_and_the_council_-_elements_for_a_new_eu_strategy_on_china.pdf.

21. House of Commons Library, "Geographical pattern of UK trade". 13 December 2024. https://commonslibrary.parliament.uk/research-briefings/cbp-7593/; Matthew Ward, "Foreign direct investment statistics". House of Commons Library, 9 December 2024. https://researchbriefings.files.parliament.uk/documents/CBP-8534/CBP-8534.pdf.

22. "Theresa May's Brexit speech in full: the prime minister outlines her twelve objectives for negotiations". *The Independent*, 17 January 2017. https://www.independent.co.uk/news/uk/home-news/full-text-theresa-may-brexit-speech-global-britain-eu-european-union-latest-a7531361.html.

23. Data from Carli Allen, "Chinese: a growing rival to French in UK schools?". Which School Adviser, 12 June 2023. https://whichschooladvisor.com/uk/school-news/chinese-a-growing-rival-to-french-in-uk-schools#:~:text=According%20to%20the%20official%20statistics,increase%20from%201%2C312%20in%202021.

CHAPTER 3

1. IMF World Economic Outlook data, cited at: https://en.wikipedia.org/wiki/Historical_GDP_of_China#cite_note-6 (accessed 29 January 2019).

2. "Xi Jinping has more clout than Donald Trump. The world should be wary". *The Economist*, 14 October 2017. https://www.economist.com/leaders/2017/10/14/xi-jinping-has-more-clout-than-donald-trump-the-world-should-be-wary.

3. Home Office, "New national security laws come into force". Gov.UK, 20 December 2023. https://www.gov.uk/government/news/new-national-security-laws-come-into-force.

4. These reports were discontinued from 2021.

5. Department for Internatioal Trade, "UK rises to 8th on World Bank's 'Ease of doing business' index". Gov.UK, 24 October 2019. https://www.gov.uk/government/news/uk-rises-to-8th-on-world-banks-ease-of-doing-business-index#:~:text=The%20UK%20has%20consolidated%20its,rising%20from%209th%20last%20year; "Ease of doing business in China", Trading Economics. https://tradingeconomics.com/china/ease-of-doing-business.

6. Rob Joyce, "Foreign Direct Investment: UK's project total grows as Europe's falls". Ernst & Young, press release, 11 July 2024. https://www.ey.com/en_uk/newsroom/2024/07/foreign-direct-investment-in-uk-grows-as-europe-declines.
7. Department for Business and Trade, "UK trade in numbers". Gov.UK. https://www.gov.uk/government/statistics/uk-trade-in-numbers/uk-trade-in-numbers-web-version.
8. Department of Business and Trade, "China trade and invesment fact sheet". 20 December 2024. https://assets.publishing.service.gov.uk/media/6762c99bcdb5e64b69e30769/china-trade-and-investment-factsheet-2024-12-20.pdf.
9. It should be noted that more recently a stronger line is being taken on Huawei in the UK, with demands for more stringent vetting and scrutiny of its products.
10. "China top threat to UK economic security – Dowden". BBC, 11 July 2023. https://www.bbc.co.uk/news/business-66156847.
11. National Security and Investment Act 2021. https://www.gov.uk/government/collections/national-security-and-investment-act.
12. Graham Lanktree, "UK signals potential curbs on Chinese investment amid 'derisking' push". Politico, 17 April 2024. https://www.politico.eu/article/uk-china-trade-investment-economy-national-security-rishi-sunak-joe-biden-oliver-dowden-tech/.
13. Lars Mucklejohn, "London edges closer to New York in battle for financial centre top spot". CITYam, 24 September 2024. https://www.cityam.com/london-edges-closer-to-new-york-in-battle-for-financial-centre-top-spot/.
14. Becca Cattlin, "What are the largest stock exchanges in the world?" IG. https://www.ig.com/uk/trading-strategies/what-are-the-largest-stock-exchanges-in-the-world--180905.
15. "Largest stock exchange operators worldwide as of January 2025, by market capitalization of listed companies". Statista. https://www.statista.com/statistics/270126/largest-stock-exchange-operators-by-market-capitalization-of-listed-companies/ (accessed 19 March 2025).
16. City of London, *London RMB Business Bi-Annual Report*. May 2024. https://www.cityoflondon.gov.uk/assets/Business/london-rmb-biannual-may-2024.pdf.
17. See Kent G. Deng, "A swinging pendulum: the Chinese way in growth and development from 1800 to the present day", in David Kerr (ed.), *China's Many Dreams: Comparative Perspectives on China's Search for National Rejuvenation* (London: Palgrave Macmillan, 2015), 97. This quote omits

the dates of the individuals named. See also Kerry Brown, "China offers an excellent trade in ideas, not just goods and services", *South China Morning Post*, 16 July 2015, https://www.scmp.com/comment/insight-opinion/article/1840220/china-offers-excellent-trade-ideas-not-just-goods-and.

18. See Willy Lam, *China in the Era of Xi Jinping* (Abingdon: Routledge, 2016).

19. "Rankings of universities in China". Wikipedia, https://en.wikipedia.org/wiki/Rankings_of_universities_in_China (accessed 19 March 2025).

20. "Open access uptake by countries/regions". STM. https://stm-assoc.org/oa-dashboard/oa-dashboard-2024/open-access-uptake-by-countries-regions/#:~:text=Authors%20based%20in%20China%20continue,and%20the%20UK%2C%203%25.

21. "List of countries by number of scientific and technical journal articles". Wikipedia, https://en.wikipedia.org/wiki/List_of_countries_by_number_of_scientific_and_technical_journal_articles (accessed 19 March 2025).

22. "Patents by country/number of patents per country 2025". World Population Review. https://worldpopulationreview.com/country-rankings/patents-by-country.

23. Ryan Hooper, "Sir Iain Duncan Smith accuses top universities of being 'in hock' to China by stifling debate for fear of losing funding". *Mail On Sunday*, 10 March 2024. https://www.dailymail.co.uk/news/article-13180331/iain-duncan-smith-china-universities.html.

24. Anne Mckie, "Chinese students in UK 'report increased racism and discrimination'". *Times Higher Educational Supplement*, 7 May 2020. https://mail.google.com/mail/u/0/#inbox.

25. Jo Johnson *et al.*, "The China Question". The Policy Institute, King's College London. March 2021. https://www.kcl.ac.uk/policy-institute/assets/china-question.pdf.

26. Vivian Moxham-Hall and Niall Sreenan, "China–UK: new report reveals massive increase in research collaboration and dependence on Chinese students". The Conversation, 15 March 2021. https://theconversation.com/china-uk-new-report-reveals-massive-increase-in-research-collaboration-and-dependence-on-chinese-students-157010.

CHAPTER 4

1. For a discussion of this issue, see Kerry Brown, *China Incorporated* (London: Bloomsbury Academic, 2022).

2. "Document 9: A ChinaFile Translation". ChinaFile, 8 November 2013. https://www.chinafile.com/document-9-chinafile-translation.

3. "UK trade with China: 2021". British Office of National Statistics, 7 June 2022. https://www.ons.gov.uk/economy/nationalaccounts/balanceof payments/articles/uktradewithchina2021/2022-06-01.

4. "China exports to the United Kingdom". Trading Economics, updated January 2025. https://tradingeconomics.com/china/exports/united-kingdom.

5. "China: Trade and Investment Factsheet". Gov.UK. https://assets.publishing.service.gov.uk/media/6762c99bcdb5e64b69e30769/china-trade-and-investment-factsheet-2024-12-20.pdf.

6. Ou Fei, "China–UK green cooperation: a promising future". *Global Times*, 29 May 2024. https://www.globaltimes.cn/page/202405/1313234.shtml.

7. Toby Ord, *The Precipice* (London: Hachette, 2021).

8. "The next frontier for AI in China could add $600 billion to its economy". McKinsey, 7 June 2022. https://www.mckinsey.com/capabilities/quantumblack/our-insights/the-next-frontier-for-ai-in-china-could-add-600-billion-to-its-economy.

9. "UK AI investment on track for record-breaking year". Fintech Finance News, 16 July 2024. https://ffnews.com/newsarticle/fintech/uk-ai-investment-on-track-for-record-breaking-year/.

10. The Bletchley Declaration by Countries Attending the AI Safety Summit, 1–2 November 2023. https://www.gov.uk/government/publications/ai-safety-summit-2023-the-bletchley-declaration/the-bletchley-declaration-by-countries-attending-the-ai-safety-summit-1-2-november-2023.

11. "Vice President Mike Pence's remarks on the administration's policy towards China". Hudson Institute, 4 October 2018. https://www.hudson.org/events/1610-vice-president-mike-pence-s-remarks-on-the-administration-s-policy-towards-china102018.

12. "Theresa May hails 'first step' to trade deal after Xi Jinping talks". BBC, 1 February 2018. https://www.bbc.co.uk/news/uk-politics-42897705.

13. "What is the China Research Group?" China Research Group News. https://chinaresearchgroup.substack.com/about.

14. Hansard, "Security Threat from China". Volume 748: debated on Monday 15 April 2024. UK Parliament. https://hansard.parliament.uk/commons/2024-04-15/debates/7767B6DD-923E-4C07-82EF-986A448606D4/SecurityThreatFromChina.

15. Tim Baker, "China 'trying to undermine our democracy' – as MPs set to be warned about new cyber attacks". Sky News, 25 March 2024. https://news.sky.com/story/china-trying-to-undermine-our-democracy-as-mps-set-to-be-warned-about-new-cyber-attacks-13101022.

16. "We should be in a stand-off with China, says Iain Duncan Smith". *Business Matters*, 7 May 2024. https://bmmagazine.co.uk/news/we-should-be-in-a-stand-off-with-china-says-iain-duncan-smith/.

17. Pak Yiu, "China's Xi says Hong Kong 'cannot afford chaos' after 2019 protests". Nikkei, 1 July 2022. https://asia.nikkei.com/Politics/China-s-Xi-says-Hong-Kong-cannot-afford-chaos-after-2019-protests.
18. Foreign, Commonwealth and Development Office, "Foreign Secretary declares breach of Sino-British Joint Declaration". 12 November 2020. https://www.gov.uk/government/news/foreign-secretary-declares-breach-of-sino-british-joint-declaration.

CHAPTER 5

1. Kerry Brown, *China in Five Cities: From Hohhot to Hong Kong* (London: ACA Publishing, 2021).
2. Michael Natzler, *Understanding China: The Study of China and Mandarin in UK Schools and Universities* (London: Higher Education Policy Institute, 2021), 23–4.
3. The British Association for Chinese Studies, *Report on the Present State of China Related Studies in the UK*. October 2021. https://bacsuk.org.uk/wp-content/uploads/2023/04/BACS-State-of-the-Field-2020-21-Report.pdf.
4. Vincent Ni, "Beijing-backed Chinese language schools in UK to be replaced with teachers from Taiwan". *The Guardian*, 18 September 2022. https://www.theguardian.com/world/2022/sep/18/beijing-backed-chinese-language-schools-in-uk-to-be-replaced-with-teachers-from-taiwan.
5. Joan Robinson, *The Cultural Revolution in China* (Harmondsworth: Penguin, 1969) is the classic statement of this.
6. See John Butler, *The Red Dean of Canterbury: The Public and Private Faces of Hewlett Johnson* (London: Scala, 2011), 195.
7. For Britain, see Tom Buchanan, *East Wind: China and the British Left, 1925 to 1976* (Oxford: Oxford University Press, 2012), and for France, Richard Wolin, *Wind from the East: French Intellectuals, the Cultural Revolution, and the Legacy of the 1960s* (Princeton, NJ: Princeton University Press, 2010).
8. "Generation UK". British Council. https://www.britishcouncil.org/partner/international-development/track-record/generation-uk.
9. Confucius, *The Analects*, trans. Arthur Waley (London: Everyman, 2000), Book XX, 3: 221.

CHAPTER 6

1. James Cleverly, "Our position on China: Foreign Secretary's 2023 Mansion House speech". Gov.UK, 25 April 2023. https://www.gov.uk/government/speeches/our-position-on-china-speech-by-the-foreign-secretary.

2. British Foreign and Development Office, "The UK and China: a framework for engagement". January 2009. https://www.lancaster.ac.uk/fass/projects/ndcc/download/uk-and-china.pdf.

3. Commission of the European Communities, "EU China: closer partners, growing responsibilities". 24 October 2006. http://trade.ec.europa.eu/doclib/docs/2006/october/tradoc_130875.pdf.

4. The "One China" policy is that whereby a country or group of countries recognize that there is only one China, and do not grant independent status to the Republic of China on Taiwan.

5. European Commission, "Joint Communication to the European Parliament and the Council: Elements for a New EU Strategy on China", 22 June 2016, 5. http://eeas.europa.eu/archives/docs/china/docs/joint_communication_to_the_european_parliament_and_the_council_-_elements_for_a_new_eu_strategy_on_china.pdf.

6. "China's crackdown on human rights lawyers". Amnesty International, 22 June 2016. https://www.amnesty.org/en/latest/campaigns/2016/07/one-year-since-chinas-crackdown-on-human-rights-lawyers/.

7. European Commission, "EU–China: a strategic outlook". https://commission.europa.eu/system/files/2019-03/communication-eu-china-a-strategic-outlook.pdf.

8. Carla Freeman, "Blinken lays out three-part U.S. approach to China. But what's missing?" United States Institute of Peace, 2 June 2022. https://www.usip.org/publications/2022/06/blinken-lays-out-three-part-us-approach-china-whats-missing.

9. "A quarter of Britons consider China to be an enemy of the UK", YouGov.

10. British Foreign Policy Group, "A UK–China engagement strategy". 22 May 2020. https://bfpg.co.uk/2020/05/intro-uk-china-strategy/.

11. "Foreign direct investment from China into the United States from 2000 to 2023". Statistica, https://www.statista.com/statistics/188935/foreign-direct-investment-from-china-in-the-united-states (accessed 19 March 2025), and "China: Trade and Investment Factsheet". Gov.UK. https://assets.publishing.service.gov.uk/media/679907671c041dcc469dae03/china-trade-and-investment-factsheet-2025-01-31.pdf.

Index